Federal Husband

Federal Husband

DOUGLAS WILSON

MOSCOW, IDAHO

Douglas J. Wilson, *Federal Husband*
© 1999 by Douglas J. Wilson.

Published by Canon Press, P.O. Box 8741, Moscow, ID 83843
800-488-2034 / www.canonpress.org

05 06 07 08 09 / 9 8 7 6 5

Cover design by Paige Atwood

Printed in the United States of America.

ISBN: 1-885767-51-X

Library of Congress Cataloging-in-Publication Data

Wilson, Douglas, 1953-
  Federal husband / Douglas Wilson.— Rev. ed.
     p. cm.
  ISBN 1-885767-51-X (pbk.)
  1. Husbands—Religious life. 2. Marriage—Religious aspects—
Christianity. I. Title.

  BV4528.2.F48 2004
  248.8'425—dc22

                              2004000921

ISBN-13: 978-1-885767-51-6
ISBN-10: 1-885767-51-X
   Federal Husband

Table of Contents

Prologue

Anyone who undertakes to add to the number of modern books on marriage had better have some good reason. This is particularly true if the author in question is doing it for the second time and all apparently unprovoked. One would think our interest in marriage books would be waning by this time; like the woman in the gospels, the more our doctors treat us, the worse we get.

But here is some more medicine anyway. The central theme of this book, the headship of the husband, was begun in *Reforming Marriage*, but there are at least two good reasons for bringing up the subject again.

The first is that such a subject as this admits of a great deal of development, discussion, and application. And so, as Paul wrote in another context, to write the same things is not necessarily tedious but rather safe (Phil. 3:1).

The second reason is related to the first. Federal thinking really is alien to the modern mind. We may consequently think we "have it down" because we have mastered the jargon, when all we are doing is using covenantal whitewash to cover up various kinds of covenantal ignorance or sin.

Our flesh doesn't need encouragement to be selfish. In the name of biblical teaching, many men either walk away from their responsibilities in headship for the sake of what they call "love," or they grossly twist what that headship should look like in the name of what they call "authority."

But it is not enough for husbands to love their wives. They must do it as Christ did for the Church. If Christ loved the Church as her Federal Lord, then we have a responsibility to discover what that means.

Federal Husband and Christ

What Does *Federal* Mean?

For various reasons, some of them obvious, the word *federal* is grossly misunderstood today. But our word comes from the Latin word *foedus*, which means covenant. Thus a federal union, or confederated association, should be understood as one bound by covenant oaths and loyalties. As Christian men who understand the importance of covenants in the Bible, we should set ourselves to understand the meaning of federal marriage.

Among the many words which our century has trashed (words like *awesome* or *gay*) this word *federal* most certainly heads the list. The word makes us think of big, centralized things, things which make a collectivist's heart feel warm and cozy. We slap the word on institutions so that little old ladies will deposit their money there. Nobody names his bank *Bob's Sunshine Bank*; the name must be something which exudes solidity and bigness like *First Federal Security* does.

Because our federal government has become about as uncovenantal as can be imagined, it is not surprising that we have forgotten the original import of the word. We believe that federal means centralized, or big, and could not refer in any way to any type of covenant.

But classical Protestant theology reflects the biblical teaching on this subject—it is not too much to say that this federal thinking is the backbone of historic Protestant orthodoxy. This brings to mind a distinction between classical Protestant theology and modern evangelical thinking: modern evangelicalism doesn't think and doesn't have a backbone. Because contemporary evangelical theology doesn't have a backbone, modern Christian men who are taught in terms of it find themselves without backbone also. And books like this one become necessary.

The Bible describes the relationship between Adam and the human race as a federal one. That is, God made a covenant with the entire human race, with Adam serving as the representative or covenant head of that race. Adam, as a covenant head, must be described as the federal head of our race. As we will see, this is why the Bible speaks of our loss of righteousness as occurring in Adam.

In the same way, our salvation was accomplished federally. Christ, the second Adam, was sent by God to be the Federal Head of a new race. His obedience was representative and was imputed to all His elect, who are identified as such by their faith. This is why Christ stands in a relationship with the Church which is described as one of headship. This headship is covenantal, which means that it is necessarily a federal headship.

This is all well and good, but how does it apply to husbands? The answer is that husbands are commanded to love their wives *as Christ loved the Church* (Eph. 5:25). By the very nature of the case, this means that husbands are told to model or exhibit a federal relationship to their wives. The command to husbands is to love their wives as Christ loved His bride.

This means that our theology of Christ's love will be determinative of how a Christian wife is loved. How a man understands ultimate covenantal loving will settle how *he* sets about covenantal loving. How he understands the thing to be imitated will determine how and what he imitates. If his theology is biblical (and thereby federal or covenantal), then his wife will be loved as Christ really did love the

Church. If the theology is either sub-federal or anti-covenantal, then a woman, when she is loved at all, will be loved sentimentally, not for very long, or in fits and starts.

In the modern Church, the central intellectual sin regarding marriage is one of theological definition. We want to assume that marriage is a permanent "roommate" arrangement between two individuals with certain sexual privileges included. But the Bible describes marriage as a covenant. The adulteress is one who forsakes the companion of her youth, the *covenant* of her God (Prov. 2:17). The men of Israel are rebuked because they abandoned their *covenantal* wives (Mal. 2:14). But we have thoughtlessly assumed that we could have biblical marriages without even knowing what a covenant marriage is.

Christian husbands do not need more exhortations from a vacuum. The marital need of the hour is that of doctrinal and theological definition—in particular, we need to understand covenants. At the heart of this covenantal relationship is the issue of responsibility. Whenever there is genuine federal headship, the head as representative *assumes responsibility* for the spiritual condition of the members of the covenant body, and the organic connection applies in both directions.

We are covenantal beings; we were created this way. Consider the mystery of how every human being is related. We are all cousins, which is to say, we are connected. Modern individualism wants to be blind to this interconnectedness and sees the imputation of Adam's sin to us as an affront to our rights. But in rejecting this, the salvation provided by Christ's righteousness, which is also imputed to us, is rejected as well.

Of course, husbands cannot duplicate this relation in its entirety in their relationship with their wives. Husbands are not Christ. But though we cannot duplicate it exactly, we are nonetheless commanded to imitate it and to seek to be *like* Christ in how He loved as a federal head. Because marriage is constituted as a covenantal institution and because the relation to be imitated is also covenantal, such imitation will of necessity be federal. Because the husband is the head of the wife as Christ is the head of the Church (Eph. 5:23), the love offered will be the love of a federal head.

Neglect of this truth is pervasive in the modern church. One of the most difficult things for modern men to understand is how they are responsible for their wives. Men come into a marriage pastoral counseling session with the assumption that "She has her problems," and "I have mine," and the counselor is here to help us split the difference. But the husband is responsible for *all* the problems. This is the case for no other reason than that he is the husband.

This does not mean that the wife has no personal responsibilities as an individual before God. She certainly does, just as her husband has individual responsibility. They are both private persons who stand before God. But he remains the head, and just as Christ *as the head* assumed all the responsibility for all the sins of all His people, so the husband is to assume covenant responsibility for the state of his marriage. If a husband says that he objects to this because it is not fair for him to be held responsible for the failings of another, he is really saying that he objects to the gospel. It was not "fair" for Christ to assume responsibility for our sins either. But while it may not have been fair as we define it, it was nevertheless just and merciful.

In reading these words, a husband may still be entirely unsure about what it means to "assume federal responsibility." And given the divine pattern assigned to us for imitation, it is certain that no husband has a complete understanding of what he is called to do. That is why we had better turn to the subject.

Headship and Covenant

What is a covenant? Our Bibles can be divided into two sections—the Old Testament or Old Covenant and the New Testament or New Covenant. One good indicator of the condition of the modern evangelical church can be seen in the fact that many believers do not understand *what* this refers to. What does the word *covenant* mean exactly? We must begin with a definition of covenant, and as we come to the various passages of Scripture which instruct a husband in his duties, how the definition applies will be clear: *a covenant is a solemn bond, sovereignly administered, with attendant blessings and curses.*

Scripture teaches that God has made one basic covenant with fallen men throughout history, which we may call the Covenant of Grace. In the New Testament, we see the final scriptural name for this covenant is the New Covenant. Prior to the Fall, God had made a covenant with mankind in Adam, which we have violated through our sin. Genesis tells us that Adam sinned against God personally, but Hosea tells us that Adam also sinned against God covenantally, "But like men they transgressed the covenant; there they dealt treacherously with Me" (Hos. 6:7). The word translated *men* here is the Hebrew word for *Adam*.

After the Fall, and throughout redemptive history, God has made covenants with His people. But they are not a series of disconnected covenants, as though God kept changing His mind about how to deal with men. His covenants unfold successively, and *they cannot be understood apart from one another*. This one covenant of grace was administered throughout history.

God established a covenant with Adam and Eve after their sin: "And I will put enmity between you and the woman, and between your seed and her Seed; He shall bruise your head, and you shall bruise His heel" (Gen. 3:15). We know from the New Testament that this was a messianic promise (e.g., Rom. 16:20), which means it must be understood covenantally. God established a covenant with Noah as well: "But I will establish My covenant with you; and you shall go into the ark—you, your sons, your wife, and your sons' wives with you" (Gen. 6:18). Peter clearly tells us that this was a type and that Christian baptism is the antitype (1 Pet. 3:18–22).

Most Christians are familiar with the covenant God made with Abraham: "And I will make My covenant between Me and you, and will multiply you exceedingly" (Gen. 17:2). As the New Testament tells us in many places, Abraham is the father of all who believe (Rom. 4:11). Moreover, the Bible tells us that "if you are Christ's, then you are Abraham's seed, and heirs according to the promise" (Gal. 3:29). The implications of this are profound.

The covenant with Moses did not represent a divine detour around all the other covenants—"So God heard their groaning, and God remembered His covenant with Abraham, with Isaac, and with Jacob. And God looked upon the children of Israel, and God acknowledged them" (Exod. 2:24–25). Understanding the ramifications of this passage is crucial to a proper grasp of the teaching of the New Testament.

Our problem is caused because we misunderstand the New Testament refutations of the Pharisaical distortions of the law of Moses. They are commonly assaulted with their own (heretical) terminological distortions (i.e., with words like "law"). But the contrast in the New Testament is not between Old and New; *the contrast is between Old distorted and Old fulfilled.*

God made a covenant with David: "When your days are fulfilled and you rest with your fathers, I will set up your seed after you, who will come from your body, and I will establish his kingdom" (2 Sam. 7:12–16). Who is the Christ? He is the Son of *David.*

All of these covenants were a prelude to the coming of the Christ. Believers should not think of separated pacts or contracts throughout history. The believer must think of a growing child, a fruitful tree, a bud unfolding into a flower. We must understand the organic continuity of the covenants. That continuity is found *in a Person* and reflects the solitary redemptive purpose of God from the beginning of history to the end of it, always expressed in a covenant. The Lord Jesus Christ is the Lord of the New

Covenant now (Heb. 8:6); has always been the Lord of the New Covenant (1 Cor. 10:1–13); and ministers throughout all history (Heb. 9:15).

The reason we must consider all this in a book on marriage and family is that God's dealings with His people throughout history (which are always covenantal) are set before us in the New Testament as the pattern for husbands to follow. The doctrine of male headship in marriage is set down for us in Scripture in a way which relates the whole thing to a right understanding of the divine covenantal order: "But I want you to know that the head of every man is Christ, the head of woman is man, and the head of Christ is God" (1 Cor. 11:3).

The covenantal order is plain. The head of Christ is God. This does not mean that Christ is less than God in His nature or being, but it does mean that the Father exercises authority over the Son. The Son is equal to the Father with regard to His nature; theologians describe this in terms of what is called the ontological Trinity. But with regard to how the Father and Son relate to one another, the Father has all authority. Theologians describe this in terms of what is called the economical Trinity.

Within the triune God, the Father is the economic head of the Son. This means He has authority over the Son with regard to their roles. The Son is equal with the Father in nature and being but did not consider that equality something to be grasped (Phil. 2:5–8). He submitted Himself to the will of the Father, and that submission has never been seen by any orthodox Christian as an admission of substantial inferiority to the Father.

In our modern egalitarian world, submission is always seen as a form of losing or of being inferior in some way. But we fall into this error because we no longer think in a trinitarian fashion. Submission is seen as entailing inferiority because we do not understand the deity of Christ and His full submission to the Father.

Conversely, we should be able to see how well we

understand the biblical doctrine of the Trinity by how well men and women function together in marriage. A man who has his wife under his thumb is an Arian—the heresy which subordinates Christ to the Father by declaring Him to be a created being. A man who abdicates his functional authority over his wife—one who capitulates to egalitarian feminism—is a Sabellian. This is the heresy which sees no real distinctions between the persons of the Godhead, only different names.

A man's head is Christ, and a woman's head is man. But this headship does not necessitate inferiority. Paul teaches us that a woman is a man's equal ontologically. Both male and female are created in the image of God (Gen. 1:27), and Paul emphatically declares that in Christ differences between the sexes are nonexistent.

> For you are all sons of God through faith in Christ Jesus. For as many of you as were baptized into Christ have put on Christ. There is neither Jew nor Greek, there is neither slave nor free, there is *neither male nor female*; for you are all one in Christ Jesus. And if you are Christ's, then you are Abraham's seed, and heirs according to the promise. (Gal. 3:26–29)

A man and woman living together as husband and wife live together as ontological equals. Peter requires that men live together with their wives, remembering that they are joint heirs (1 Pet. 3:7). However, in the economic realm, the husband is the head—"For the husband is head of the wife, as also Christ is head of the church; and He is the Savior of the body" (Eph. 5:23). It is worth remembering at this point that our word *economic* comes from the Greek word which means household.

Now some might want to assume that we simply have covenantal headship on the brain and therefore find it everywhere in Scripture. When a man first finds a hammer, everything looks like a nail. But this teaching is not an example of a "systematic" covenant theology running amok.

As we saw, the adulteress described in Proverbs forsook the companion of her youth, the *covenant* of her God, and the men in Malachi were chastised because of how they treated their wives by *covenant*. Further, in the language of headship, the Bible assumes a covenantal headship. Indeed, in Scripture there is no other kind of headship. So marriage is clearly described in the Bible as a covenantal institution.

But much more is involved in this than just the word. We need to take a closer look at the central scriptural paradigms for headship—the headship of Adam and Christ already mentioned. The relation that exists between us and Adam is clearly a covenantal one. Because we are organically connected to him by covenant, when he sinned in the garden, we all sinned as represented in him. He sinned covenantally and presented us to God in that rebellion— "But [like Adam] they transgressed the covenant; there they dealt treacherously with Me" (Hos. 6:7). In his sin, we sinned. But the federal headship of Adam is most clearly seen in the biblical descriptions of Christ's headship. Christ is plainly described as the Head of His people, and He is described as *being like Adam* in this regard. God in His mercy brought us out of sin the same way we were plunged into it. In the same way that the sin of the first Adam condemned us, the obedience of the second Adam rescued us. Nevertheless death reigned from Adam to Moses, even over those who had not sinned according to the likeness of the transgression of Adam, *who is a type of Him who was to come* (Rom. 5:14–15).

Paul makes the same point in his discussion of the resurrection in 1 Corinthians: "And so it is written, 'The first man Adam became a living being.' *The last Adam* became a life-giving spirit" (1 Cor. 15:45). "For as in Adam all die, *even so in Christ* all shall be made alive" (1 Cor. 15:22). Putting this together, we see that both Adam and Christ are described as the representative or covenantal heads of their respective people. This is how our sins can be imputed to Christ, and how His righteousness can be imputed to us.

In Adam, this is our condemnation. In Christ, this is our glory and salvation. And, in marriage, *this is the kind of relationship which God commands husbands to imitate.*

We must also understand what this does not mean. Before authority in marriage can be understood, we must repent of all our individualism. In marriage, we do not have two separated individuals with one of them in charge of the other one. Rather, we have an organic union which is instructed not to be schizophrenic. All macho man foolishness is inconsistent with the covenantal realities described here.

A proper understanding also excludes the blame game. A husband can no more blame his wife for the state of their marriage than a thief can blame his hands. As Christ assumed responsibility for things He didn't do, so husbands should be willing to do the same for their wives.

Obviously, sins can be committed in marriage by both men and women. But all such sinning occurs in the context of a covenant and within the realm of the federal head's responsibility. The responsibility for all such sins therefore lies with the husband. A woman can and should recognize her sins before the Lord; her husband's overarching responsibility should in no way lessen her sense of personal and individual responsibility. Properly understood, it should have precisely the opposite effect. When a wife understands that her husband is responsible and knows that he assumes this responsibility willingly, she will be more responsible as an individual, not less. In the same way that Christ's federal salvation sets a man free to do right, so a husband can liberate his wife as he assumes responsibility for her.

We frequently struggle with what we think is the conflict between such federal responsibility and personal responsibility, because the individualism of our age has taught us to think of responsibility in *either/or* terms instead of *both/and*. But the federal responsibility of the husband and the responsibility of the wife are not to be understood as separate billiard balls which cannot occupy the same place. A wife may think, "Either *he* is responsible or *I* am." Or sometimes we seek to divide the responsibility—50/50, or 70/30. But it must always, we think, add up to 100.

This is why adversarial thinking develops in a marriage. "*You* are over there, and *I* am over here, and we each have our perspective." But covenantal thinking provides the biblical basis for being able to say *we*.

Covenantal responsibility of this kind does not divide; rather, it multiplies and ascends. Federal thinking preserves the personhood of those involved; it does not annihilate that personhood. The assumption of covenantal responsibility by a husband does not diminish the personal responsibility of his wife for everything she does and thinks; rather, it strengthens it.

This mentality is not condemning but liberating—a husband who considers this knows exactly what he is supposed to do. This thing is hard but not impossible. It is simple to understand, which is good, because it is hard to do. A man must swallow his pride, which *is* hard to get down, and then stand up and do a very simple thing. Every doctrine lives as it is applied and no other way. The application of this doctrine is simply a question of having an obedient mind. *This is not a technique*; it is the *mind of wisdom*.

As Christ Loved the Church

If this book has a central refrain, it is that husbands are to love their wives as Christ loved the Church. For many Christian men this means nothing more than that Christ loved the Church "a lot" and that husbands should strive to do the same. But what it really means is that husbands should love their wives *federally*, the same way that Christ loved the Church. Given the nature of the divine love expressed on the cross, we can only *begin* to point out what this means. And when we think we are done, there will be no fewer days to talk about what we still have to learn.

First, we must recall what the Bible teaches about Christ's sacrificial love. In many ways we have trivialized our understanding of that event—tee-shirts on sale in Christian bookstores show Christ with outstretched arms saying that He loves us "this much." Here we see something happening in our midst which always happens when the theology of the cross is forgotten. When the meaning of the crucifixion is neglected, men keep their memory of the crucifixion but begin to focus on the physical aspects of it—the wounds, the flogging, the nails in His hands. The Bible is clear that Christ did suffer physically, but that was not what filled His soul with horror as He contemplated the death that was approaching Him. John tells us that Christ's heart was troubled as He considered His fate in the hands of sinful men: "Now My soul is troubled, and what shall I say? 'Father, save Me from this hour'? But for this purpose I came to this hour" (Jn. 12:27).

He was appalled at the prospect of abandonment by His Father. He knew that He was to be sin on the cross for us. He was never a sinner, but He did become covenantally *sinful* and consequently came under the judgment of God—"For He made Him who knew no sin to be sin for us, that we might become the righteousness of God in Him" (2 Cor. 5:21). This is why Christ called out in despair—"And at the ninth hour Jesus cried out with a loud voice, saying, 'Eloi, Eloi, lama sabachthani?' which is translated, 'My God, My God, why have You forsaken Me?'" (Mk. 15:34). In the atonement, Christ was smitten by *God* and afflicted.

Apart from a federal or covenantal union of Christ with His people, none of this makes any kind of moral sense. If one man is guilty of a heinous crime, how does it comport with justice to kill someone else for that crime? If we hasten to explain that the substituted victim was entirely righteous and had never done anything wrong, this only makes it *worse*, not better.

If Christ were merely a perfect individual and we a collection of imperfect individuals, then what is declared by us to be the gospel would actually be a moral monstrosity. Because God is good, His substitutionary death for His people must have a just ground for that substitution. Apart from genuine union with Christ, the execution of one man over here for the sins of those men over there is appalling. But the union we have with Christ is described in the Bible as the union of an Adam with His nation, a federal head with His people. The Bible knows nothing of any other kind of union of Christ with His people. This is why the cross is a display of justice and not a monstrosity. This is why God in the cross was able to be both just *and* the One who justifies (Rom. 3:26).

Now when this understanding of the cross is neglected, as it has been in our day, this does not mean that the fact of the cross is forgotten. The sentimentalism described earlier takes over, and it is uniformly drawn out by emphasizing the physical anguish of Christ on the cross. That anguish is presented in the Bible, but it is presented in the figure of speech called *synecdoche*, where a part may be presented for the whole. "Many hands make light work," but we all know that whole people have to be attached to those hands. The word *hands* stands in for and represents those people. In the same way, we are redeemed by the blood of Christ (Eph. 1:7). His blood, His wounds, represent for us *everything* He did for us on the cross—the shedding of His blood to the point of death while He hung on a tree under the curse of God. Christ redeemed us from the curse of the law by becoming a curse for us (Gal. 3:13). This *becoming a curse* is essential to understand. How might an innocent man become a curse for a guilty man? The question cannot be answered apart from covenantal union.

Now a husband is also in covenantal union with his wife. He is instructed to behave in that union with the mind of Christ. We can perhaps see how important this is if we were to attribute to Christ all the various things which husbands do. A man who is the head of his wife is preaching all day about Christ and the Church—his obedience or disobedience will determine whether his preaching is full of lies or not, but the very nature of his relation to his wife means that he *is* preaching, like it or not.

Picture Christ murmuring against His wife to the Father, "The woman Thou gavest . . ." Imagine Christ blaming the Church, pointing an accusing finger. Try to picture Christ wishing that He were with someone else. Every situation we might come up with piles absurdity on absurdity. When a man learns this and begins to treat his wife in a manner consistent with that insight, he soon sees the difference between sentimental attachments and covenantal identity.

Christ loved His bride with an efficacious love; He loved the Church in a way which transformed her. In the same way a husband is to assume responsibility for his wife's increasing loveliness. One man marries a pretty woman and hopes, fingers crossed, that she will manage to stay that way. But a federal husband marries a beautiful woman and vows before God and witnesses that he will nourish and cherish her in such a way that she flourishes in that beauty. Christ bestowed loveliness on His Church through His love. A Christian man is called to do the same. Covenant loving bestows loveliness. Federal commitment imparts beauty.

Christ's love was also an incarnational love. The Word did not love the Church from a great distance. Rather, He took on the form of a servant and emptied Himself. Christ's love for His Church was literally *embodied* in His sacrificial life. His love was not measured by what He *felt*; it was measured by what He accomplished. Of course, what He accomplished was what He desired to do, but the Bible forbids the detachment of intentions and behavior. Love should be defined as lawful behavior from the heart. We want to separate the two, letting tight-shoed Pharisees have the lawful behavior and letting the mystical goo churches have the heart.

The love of Christ is defined in terms of what He did,

and what He did, He did with a whole heart. In the same way, husbands are to love their wives with this same kind of incarnational love. This is related to Paul's instruction to men requiring them to love their wives as their own bodies: "So husbands ought to love their own wives as their own bodies; he who loves his wife loves himself" (Eph. 5:28).

A man does not care for his own body sporadically. As Paul puts it, no one ever hated his own flesh. Imagine a man taking his body out to a restaurant only on its birthday, and giving it a present only on its anniversary. No, a man's relationship with his body is much more . . . *ongoing*. A man deals with his own body in one way or another every minute of every day. And when a man does what Paul requires here, he loves his wife in this same ongoing, incarnational way.

As discussed earlier, Christ loved His people with a responsible love. In His loving, He took on Himself all the sins of His people. These were sins which He had not personally committed and for which we had no right to blame Him. And yet, on the basis of the covenant union, He assumed responsibility. The ground of our salvation is nothing less than Christ's assumption of that responsibility.

In the same way, a husband may not be to blame for a particular problem in his marriage. But whether he is at fault or not, he remains responsible. Christ was never to blame for anything that God held Him responsible for, and yet He assumed the responsibility for all our sins. You would think that we as husbands who *do* share so much of the blame would find it easier to assume the responsibility. But the flesh revolts, and we do not want to take an ounce of responsibility over the measure of our blame—and frequently, we want even less than that. Another way of saying this is that husbands don't want to love their wives the way the Bible tells them to.

Put simply, the husband and wife are both private persons and are each individually responsible for what they do. When the husband sins, he must confess the sin. When the wife sins, she must confess the sin. But this individual confession does not cover the corporate aspect of marriage. The couple together are a corporate person. So in addition to being a private person, the husband is also a public person; he is vested with an office. He has an invisible husbandly robe which he wears, and in that office, he bears the responsibility for the spiritual state of the family. His name as a private person is William. Her name as a private person is Susan. His name as a public person is Smith, and, in this sense of representation and responsibility, *he is the Smiths*.

Lastly, Christ loved His people with an instructional love. Christ washed His Church with the Word, as should husbands. The Lord is not only our priest and king, He is also the prophet who instructs His people. In Paul's teaching, he requires the husband to teach his wife in the same way. He is not told to pile on the information; he is told to wash his wife with the water of the Word "that He might sanctify and cleanse her with the washing of water by the word" (Eph. 5:26).

Paul presupposes that husbands will be equipped to answer the questions of their wives, "And if they [the wives] want to learn something, let them ask their own husbands at home" (1 Cor. 14:35). Many contemporary women might wonder at this: "Why should I ask him? *He* doesn't know!" This is because men have neglected the charge which Scripture gives to all husbands. Men believe that they do not have to know because they believe they have no responsibilities of instruction. But as Christ cleanses the Church with the Word of God, so husbands are to do the same to their wives.

This must always be done in the context of the substitutionary atonement of Christ. Whenever religious teaching is detached from the sacrifice of Christ on the cross, it always degenerates into a vapid moralism. And when husbands instruct their wives without the framework of the atonement shaping their thinking, their instruction will exhibit only a pious cast of mind with the edges of each word smudged and blurred.

More frequently, when husbands lose an understanding of the cross, they come to the point where they do not instruct their wives in the Word at all. Of course, as the head of the wife, an ignorant husband continues to teach, but the lessons have to do with how Christ is more interested in Monday Night Football than in communion with His bride.

Not Where They Should Be

But how does federal headship work in messier situations? Perhaps a couple marry when both were non-Christians, and he later becomes a Christian. Perhaps he was a believer who disobediently married an unbeliever. He repents later, but he obviously remains married. Perhaps husband and wife are both professing believers, but through his abdication of godly authority, she has backslidden to the point that he simply does not know if he is capable of leading her. Most married Christian men are not in this position, but at the same time, we cannot say the problem is extremely rare.

The symptoms can of course vary. He may be distressed over her spending habits, television viewing habits, weight, rejection of his leadership, laziness in cleaning the house, lack of responsiveness to sexual advances—whatever. But however the problem is manifested, what should a husband do? Suppose for a moment that he really wants to serve God in their marriage, and she appears to be distinctly rebellious about changing any of her ways. What course should a man pursue?

First, the husband in his capacity as a private person should confess to God his own sins as an individual which have contributed to the situation. For the typical husband, such sins will be numerous and may even include the initial decision to marry her. In other words, to take an example at random, if his name is Jay, he begins by confessing Jay's sins.

Second, the husband as a "public person" should begin confessing the sinful state of his household before God, assuming full and complete responsibility for the way things are. Remember that the husband is an individual, but he is also an officer—he is invested with the office of husband. In this status, he is not his own man; he is a public person—he represents others. The responsibilities of a public person are not the same thing as the guilt of a private person. When a wife neglects her duties, the guilt of the sin is hers. The responsibility for her negligence is her husband's.

The husband should therefore confess, on a daily basis, the sinful status of his household before God and his responsibility for it, until it changes. A "problem wife" cannot be worked on like a car that has broken down. Because of the organic and covenantal nature of marriage, the problem is never "over there, with *her*," but rather here "with *us*." And who is the spokesman for "us," the spokesman for this particular household before God? The husband is, and he must learn the importance of such corporate confession. If his name is Jay Smith, he must learn to confess the Smiths' sins, and he must do so as the covenant representative of that household.

Third, when he has learned to assume full responsibility before God for the spiritual condition of the household (and not before then) and the ramifications of this lesson have settled in his marrow, the husband should then sit down and have a talk with his wife. In this talk, he must assume the complete responsibility for the way things are. The chances are that he has previously blamed her many times, both in his heart and out loud, and this is not to be a sanctimonious version of the same thing. While granting the reality of her negligence and her individual guilt before the Lord, his talk should not be accusing. After he has acknowledged his responsibility and his failures to exercise it properly, he should then make clear what his expectations are for her in the future. He should also make clear his complete unwillingness to step in to do for her what she neglected to do or to tolerate a lapse into the old way of doing things.

Fourth, his expectations for change should not be exhaustive but rather representative. He should want to address the problem in principle, not *in toto*. The purpose of this discussion is not to present a twenty-year-old list of grievances—love does not keep a record of wrongs—but rather to help her learn to do her duty and to lead her as she learns what is, for her, a difficult lesson. She can learn on a representative problem. She would be overwhelmed with a requirement that she change everywhere, all at once. If, for example, the problem is one of poor housekeeping, he should require something very simple, i.e., that the dishes be done after every meal before anything else is done.

The first time the dishes are not done, he must sit down with his wife immediately and gently remind her that this is something which has to be done. At no time may he lose his temper, badger her, call her names, etc. He must constantly remember and confess that she is not the problem, he is. By bringing this gently to her attention, he is not to be primarily pointing to her need to repent; rather, he is exhibiting the fruit of his repentance.

He does this, without rancor and without an accusative spirit, until she complies or rebels. If she complies, he must move up one step, now requiring that another of her duties be done. If she continues to rebel after patient effort, he should at some point call the elders of the church and ask them for a pastoral visit. When the government of the home has failed to such an extent and a godly and consistent attempt by the husband to restore the situation has broken down, then the involvement of the elders is fully appropriate.

Federal Husband Against Himself

Seeing the Back of Your Head

The Word of God is given to us in order to enable us to see ourselves. When we examine our own hearts, there is much we cannot see. This is why introspection is not the route to self-knowledge but to confusion. The study of God's Word is the only proper way to come to a proper understanding of ourselves. And in order to see ourselves properly, we always have to hold up the mirror of the Word—"For if anyone is a hearer of the word and not a doer, he is like a man observing his natural face in a mirror; for he observes himself, goes away, and immediately forgets what kind of man he was" (Jas. 1:23).

When we hold the Scriptures up in this way, God enables us to see things we do not normally see—i.e., the back of our own spiritual head. In particular, husbands may begin to see their responsibilities scripturally defined, as well as some of the common sins which husbands frequently commit.

Scripture will sometimes teach us in an offhand way. When Paul requires husbands to love their wives as Christ loved the Church, he is not exactly making an indirect point. But Scripture will frequently teach through the assumptions that are clearly made in a passage which is primarily addressing something else.

An example of this can be found in Exodus 21:10 in a law regulating and restricting polygamy: "If he takes another wife, he shall not diminish her food, her clothing, and her marriage rights." In other words, in this situation, a husband was only permitted to take a second wife if he did not cease certain fundamental marital duties with regard to his first wife. Those marital duties were respectively, conjugal relations, provision of clothing, and provision of food.

The Bible is the Word of God, but it must be admitted that the spiritual words of Scripture frequently take a far more mundane turn than we might expect. One should not really be all that surprised to find the author of Proverbs, for example, exhorting us to change our oil every three thousand miles or to rotate our tires. We are tempted to think of such things as not really high-minded enough for Scripture because we are more gnostic than Christian in our thinking. The biblical understanding is that the earth is the Lord's and everything in it. The gnostic view is that spiritual things are always "up" and out of reach, or "in" and out of touch. What matters is emphatically *not* what happens here and now. The scriptural requirement is quite different from this.

Consider the requirements of the above law. A man has a basic responsibility before God to make love to his wife regularly, keep her cupboards full, and to do the same to her closet. This is not quite the "love her forever and a day" violin stuff that we have come to expect from some Christian romance-as-the-foundation-for-marriage seminars.

Now some might counter that this neglects the fact that we are discussing a requirement from a law dealing with polygamy. So it is, but we should argue *a fortiori* from this. If a *polygamist* was required by God to do these things for his first wife, how much more should a monogamist meet the same standard? We do not want to find ourselves in the position of arguing that now in the Christian era, with monogamy set forth as the norm for God's people (1 Tim. 3:2; Eph. 5:25), God has in His infinite wisdom restricted us to one woman so that we could learn to treat her more poorly than was required under the Old Covenant. A man must love his wife as Christ loved the church. But this does not refer to any divine expectation that we send our emotions off hang-gliding. It refers to an efficacious *and very mundane* provision. That provision is to be what God requires, and we must supply it in the way God requires. A man may effectively fall away from the faith through his failure to do so—"But if anyone does not provide for his own, and especially for those of his household, he has denied the faith and is worse than an unbeliever" (1 Tim. 5:8).

The duty of ongoing sexual relations is clearly presented by Paul when he says, "Let the husband render to his wife the affection due her, and likewise also the wife to her husband" (1 Cor 7:3). Modern liberated types enjoy sniffing at this, as though making sexual relations a duty somehow removes the romance, the excitement, the Original Flame. The thing that will supposedly carry us through to the end of our lustful little lives is supposed to be that spontaneous combustion thing between man and woman, like in those movies they make nowadays for heavy breathers. But any pastor who knows what it is like to counsel a couple who cannot even touch one another any more, knows what a bogus help this doctrine of spontaneous romance is. And our generation, riddled as it is with divorce, ought to be a little more humble about giving out advice concerning long-term sexual contentment.

Men also need to learn self-denial as they provide for their wives in nonsexual ways. The joke that the difference between men and boys is the price of their toys contains more truth than is good for us. Far too many men have never withheld from themselves toys (guns, boats, dirt bikes, fishing gear, etc.), and yet their wives have to struggle to set the table or to dress themselves. When this is the case, such men are falling short of God's standard.

Christian men must see to it that these fundamental duties are discharged. This cannot be done by "letting" her get a job so that she can help provide. Many excuses are offered up in our greedy and discontented age ("It takes two paychecks nowadays"), which will enable us to send the wives off to help provide for themselves. But if a man is not capable of providing his wife with food and clothing, then he is scripturally disqualified to be a husband. He has no right to get married. In a time when many women are more qualified to take a wife than many men are, it is not surprising that gender confusion is rampant.

But biblical stewardship of finances is never fulfilled through strewing money about. An important corollary must be connected to all of this. If a man has a wife who is not as responsible as she should be in her purchase of food and clothing, he is responsible to oversee her financial dealings. A man may be a poor provider through thoughtless abundance as much as through lack of provision. But if he serves God with both his hands, then his work is received as spiritual worship, both good and acceptable. He does this as he meets her needs in all three areas. When these responsibilities are neglected, certain common sins recur. One obvious sin is that of refusing to take responsibility. As we have already seen, the man is the head of the woman (1 Cor. 11:3). His only option therefore is whether he will accept this or refuse to face the fact. Many Christian men refuse, and it shows in their marriages.

Related to this is the refusal to be masculine. In 1 Corinthians 16:13, Paul charges the Corinthians to be courageous in their sanctification. The word he uses literally means to *act the man*. Especially in the arena of marriage, men need to learn to be men.

Another sin is that of mental infidelity. Jesus's words are well-known: "But I say to you that whoever looks at a woman to lust for her has already committed adultery with her in his heart" (Mt. 5:28). This includes, but is not limited to, lust provoked by magazines, co-workers, daughters and wives of friends, Internet images, movies, songs, daydreams, or anything else you might be able to come up with.

Some husbands are guilty of harsh bitterness. Paul goes out of his way to tell husbands that love includes a refusal to be embittered by the behavior of their wives (Col. 3:19). Other men opt for the old-fashioned sin of being a blockhead. Not to overstate it, women are complicated beings. This is why Peter requires husbands to treat their wives *according to knowledge* (1 Pet. 3:7). The Word of God does not permit a man to fail this course. Men must *study* their wives, and they must do so according to what God has revealed in His Word.

Treat Her Like a Lady

As difficult as the concept is for males to understand, feminine weakness is not a weakness. No woman should ever be evaluated apart from her creation design or divinely-appointed purpose. Neither should any man. God has made each of us, male and female, for a particular calling and has equipped us for that calling. As the calling varies, so does the equipping.

Because one of the male strengths is simple-mindedness, men tend to evaluate all things according to the sort of criterion (fixed in their minds sometime in junior high) best illustrated by arm-wrestling contests or a footrace. Life is simple—stronger and faster is better. And because life is also a contest, everyone is measured by whether or not he or she is "winning" it. Unfortunately, more than a few foolish women have been sucked into this mindset. And ironically, we call this attempt by some women to be more like men "feminism," which is more than a little bit like calling an attempt by cats to be like dogs *felinism*.

When such attempts don't work, which they haven't, we careen off in another direction. So our egalitarian age is currently insisting, for some reason, that we now learn to respect "diversity," but it can give no coherent reason, given its relativistic premises, why we should do so. Without confidence in God's creation design, we have no reason to respect anything, much less diversity. The modern feminist

whines that we should all come to respect her distinctives
after her decades-long attempts to obliterate them, her re-
peated attempts to compete with men on their own terms,
as well as her losing badly in many such attempts. One response could be that we will respect her distinctives when
she does. We will bow when she learns to curtsey.

But such an attitude is appropriate only for those women
who have abandoned home-orientation in exchange for that
great modern privilege of dumping the kids off at day care.
The biblically wise woman laughs at any such attempts to
turn women inside out. A woman's station is honored and
respected in Scripture and should be honored by all Christians as well. The fifth commandment requires that children honor their parents. The father's responsibility is to
see that this general commandment is honored in its particular applications. One of the most important applications
is that of honoring the mother of the home.

Children are of course to honor both father and mother.
This is a commandment with a promise; parents who care
about their children will insist that children learn to keep
this command (Eph. 6:1–4). This is done not because the
parents are power-tripping but because they are seeking
God's blessing for their offspring. An important part of
teaching this lesson—particularly to sons—is the respect
and honor which a husband demonstrates to his wife in the
presence of their children. Inescapably, children learn by
the example set by their parents. We may provide them
with a good example or a bad example, but we never have
the option of providing "no example."

A husband should never speak to his wife as though
she were one of the children. A condescending attitude is
completely out of place. Neither should he undercut her
decisions in front of the kids or dispute with her or
demean her in any way. If discussion of a disagreement is
absolutely necessary, it should take place away from the
children. The father should insist that the parents constantly
present a united front to the children. I am overstating the

point for didactic purposes, but sometime around the age of sixteen, the children should realize that their parents are actually two people. The father should take the lead in gratitude. He should lead the family on complimenting her on her meals, on her appearance, and for the work she does in keeping the home running smoothly. He should be saying "thank you" many times each day, and he should insist that his children learn to follow his example.

A man must insist that his children honor those whom he honors, and the first one on this list should be his wife and their mother. I still recall that when I was a child my father laid out three cardinal sins that we as children could commit—they were "lying, disobedience, and disrespecting your mother" respectively. Now honor means much more than the mere absence of disrespect, but some of the best teaching moments on the duty of honoring mother come at the points of discipline for disrespecting her.

As will be developed in a later chapter, a man should teach his children the loveliness of pregnancy. Our generation has a pathological hatred of the womb, as evidenced by our abortion culture's imbecility with regard to children. The alternative understanding should be set forth in Christian homes where a man honors his wife with child, her waiting breasts full of grace thinly disguised as milk. When a woman has "gotten a child," the radiance of her complexion given to her by the Lord should be noticed and praised by her husband. Her husband must honor her fruitfulness. When a man honors his wife in all these respects, and many others unmentioned, he is really doing two things. He is teaching his children respect for their mother, and in addition, he is instilling in them a high respect for the other half of the commandment. They learn to respect him. He does this by giving, not demanding. He does this by serving, not grasping. A man who insists on respect and honor for his wife is clearly an honorable man himself. A man rarely stands taller than when he stands for a lady.

Such respect for women is not a capitulation to feminism but rather the only antidote to it. Lack of discernment in Christian circles concerning the true nature of feminism is currently pandemic. As a result, certain "masculinist" responses to feminism, which only reflect that confusion, are offered to us.

Masculinist Reactions

About the only assault against us which we are capable of understanding is the overt assault with a meat ax. If an organization were formed dedicated to "the abolition of marriage as we know it and the execution of all available males," Christians with "traditional values" would see the danger, mobilize, and fight, sometimes effectively.

But even then, about ten years later, many Christians would quietly adopt the central premise of their enemies and begin peddling this new innovation as "just what the church today needs" if we are to be "relevant" and communicate the gospel "effectively in the modern world." Compromise and unnecessary capitulation would be whooped as though they were victory. *Down* would be marketed as though it were *up*. The quest for relevance would ensure that concerns for truth would be quietly dropped.

Feminism is a very dangerous teaching, but part of its danger can be seen in its versatility and subtlety. This is why a quiet adoption of feminism is happening in two different kinds of masculinist responses to feminism. One is typified by the Promise Keeper approach to masculine renewal. But it is also happening in the "neo-Amish" home-centered reaction to modernity. Each movement, in its own way, has made a secret peace with feminism and is quietly advancing the heart of the feminist agenda. This is not being done consciously or overtly, but it is most clearly happening.

The central premise, which has been adopted by both movements, is that the feminine perspective, whatever it may happen to be, is normative. On the left side of the evangelical mainstream, this happens when men are taught how to relate to other men the way women relate to one another. This is a common problem with the Promise Keeper approach to the inculcation of masculinity. Men gather together in small groups in order to learn how to relate to one another on a more intimate level. In other words, they gather together to learn to relate to one another as women relate to each other. "Real" masculinity is described as being sensitive, open, responsive, intimate, caring, and the rest of it. (About the only thing that is missing is breast implants.)

This is because men who have been masculine and ungodly are led to confuse the two and drop the masculinity in order to become more godly. But when a man sins, he sins like a man. The solution is to deal with the sin and not with the "like a man" part. The response to masculine sinning should not be effeminacy but rather a masculine approach to godliness.

But there is always a ditch on both sides of the road. On the reactionary right, in the traditionalist reaction to modernity, we can see the same pattern. The woman's perspective on the home and family is accepted as normative and binding on all members of the family. Because she is home-centered, everyone else must be too. When women thought they belonged out in the workplace, off they went, and many men meekly went along with the experiment. Now many women have decided that the workplace is not for them (including not a few strident secular feminists), so they have decided to go home again. But among many traditionalist Christians, the women have decided that the men must go along with them. Many men have, meekly submitting once again. But as the men adopt the home-centered vision which God intended only for wives, they have in fact betrayed their wives.

The problem, as always, is masculine abdication. In the very common vacuum of leadership, certain books setting forth this home-centered paradise are often circulated by women to women, and then discontented wives urge their husbands to "come on home." In practice, this works out in the teaching that men must work at home, or out of their homes, and that only "family business" is legitimate. A man who leaves in a car and spends the day at the office is thought to be compromising with the spirit of the age.

Now in this it is important to emphasize that there is no problem with men who *happen* to work out of a shop at their home or with men who farm the piece of ground next to the house. The problem is not in what men do; the problem is in the *why*. If a man works at a family business because it is something he believes God has called him to do, then well and good. But if he believes that such home-centered work is biblically *mandatory*, then he has missed the teaching of Scripture. Of course, by the same token, if a man heads off to the office simply because he was instructed by modernity to do so, then he is not conforming his work to the pattern of Scripture either.

Only biblical teaching is normative. The masculine perspective is not normative for marriage and family, and neither is the feminine perspective. Neither traditionalism nor modernity have authority; only the commandments of God have this. God created men and women with different orientations, and He is the only one with the authority to make the assignments. The woman's assigned orientation is toward the home. The husband is supposed to lead his wife in this orientation and support her in it as she supports him. But as he loves her, he is not supposed to *share* her orientation.

In the teaching of the Bible, we see many examples of vocations which are lawful and which take a man outside and away from the home. This is initially seen in the creation ordinance and in the apostle Paul's comment on it. Adam was created to tend the garden and to exercise dominion over the earth. Eve was created to help him do this. In other words, her creation was subordinate to his, and her divinely appointed task was to help him fulfill his mission. In order to do this, women are instructed to be "discreet, chaste, homemakers, good, obedient to their own husbands, that the word of God may not be blasphemed" (Titus 2:5). She does this because she was created for *him* and not the other way around—"Nor was man created for the woman, but woman for the man" (1 Cor. 11:9). Numerous lawful vocations cannot be centered on the home. Nevertheless, men employed in such callings need a home in order for them to serve God effectively. For example, Cornelius was a soldier (Acts 10:1–2) and a devout, holy man. Erastus was a city treasurer (Rom. 16:23) and a Christian brother. He probably did not have a personal computer so that he could do his work from home. The excellent woman in Proverbs 31 is the manager of the home; she is not afraid of snow for her household (v. 21). This would not be the case if her husband were at home, supervising her work, or following her to the supermarket, telling her what can of beans to buy. He is where he is supposed to be, away from home, sitting in the gates with the elders of the city (v. 23).

Again, this is not directed at men who may have an office at home or who may share in the work of home education. There are many good practical reasons why a particular family business could and should operate out of the home successfully. But those men who have accepted the home-centered vision for men *as a necessary biblical requirement* deserve the strongest rebuke—not because of their traditionalist masculinity, but for just the opposite problem of effeminate abdication.

Of course we must never praise those men who spend so much time away from home that they give their children one mother and no father. But reaction is no solution at all. We should not praise those men who go home to try to give their children two mothers either. This is nothing less than the cleaned-up traditionalist version of Heather and her two mommies.

The problem is much greater than one of a simple mistake. The errors here are wrapped in so many confusions that apart from a remarkable intervention of God's grace, the Christian home in our nation will fall beyond recovery. What calls itself "masculine" today, isn't. And what calls itself masculine recovery today, isn't. Suppose the ladies started recovering their femininity by chewing tobacco?

Masculine Signs

We are accustomed to our relativistic and androgynous belief that cultural displays of masculinity and femininity are infinitely flexible. Like all falsehoods, this is made more plausible by the measure of truth it possesses. Certain distinctives between the sexes *are* culturally relative, but it is a *non sequitur* to reason that all distinctives fall in the same category.

The notion of "manliness" is easily mocked and consequently is defended only with difficulty. The purpose of this section is to discuss the outward trappings of masculinity with three areas of discussion—clothing, hair, and jewelry. We live in an androgynous culture, and the world around us is laboring mightily to get us to blur every distinction between the sexes that we can. The task of the Christian husband and father is to keep those things from blurring in his own manner of life and teach his family well.

Clothing: We must fix it in our minds that there is no neutrality *anywhere*. Relativism is dangerous in all its guises. This is true of our clothes, and it goes far beyond simple things like modesty. The modern view of clothing is that anything goes, as long as there is a swoosh on it somewhere.

But the way a man dresses can indicate his spiritual condition—"And Jacob said to his household and to all who were with him, 'Put away the foreign gods that are among you, purify yourselves, *and change your garments*'" (Gen. 35:2). A more drastic example can be seen with Legion: "And when He stepped out on the land, there met Him a certain man from the city who had demons for a long time. And he wore *no clothes*, nor did he live in a house but in the tombs" (Lk. 8:27). Not surprisingly, our salvation is pictured in terms of clothing: "Awake, awake! Put on your strength, O Zion; put on *your beautiful garments*, O Jerusalem, the holy city! For the uncircumcised and the unclean shall no longer come to you" (Is. 52:1). A few chapters later, Isaiah reiterates the point, "To console those who mourn in Zion, to give them beauty for ashes, the oil of joy for mourning, *the garment of praise* for the spirit of heaviness; that they may be called trees of righteousness, the planting of the Lord, that He may be glorified" (Is. 61:3).

In countless places, Scripture refers to men reflecting their sorrow and grief through their clothing: "Then Jacob tore his clothes, put sackcloth on his waist, and mourned for his son many days" (Gen. 37:34). Sometimes this was done publicly, and sometimes it was simply before the Lord: "Now it happened, when the king heard the words of the woman, that he tore his clothes; and as he passed by on the wall, the people looked, and there underneath he had *sackcloth on his body*" (2 Kgs. 6:30).

Conversely, clothes are used to reflect a release from mourning: "So David arose from the ground, washed and anointed himself, and *changed his clothes*; and he went into the house of the Lord and worshiped. Then he went to his own house; and when he requested, they set food before him, and he ate" (2 Sam. 12:20).

On a festive occasion, like a wedding, clothing is important: "But when the king came in to see the guests, he saw a man there who did not have on *a wedding garment*. So he said to him, 'Friend, how did you come in here without *a wedding garment?*' And he was speechless" (Mt. 22:11–12). Isaiah understood the difference between party clothes and blue jeans—"the *festal apparel*, and the mantles; the outer garments, the purses" (Is. 3:22). The Preacher of Ecclesiastes understood the same—"Let your *garments* always be

white, and let your head lack no oil" (Eccl. 9:8).
Clothing reveals societal status: "She shall put off *the
clothes of her captivity*, remain in your house, and mourn
her father and her mother a full month; after that you may
go in to her and be her husband, and she shall be your wife"
(Deut. 21:13).

When Tamar deceived her father-in-law, she did it in
part by means of her clothing: "So she took off *her widow's
garments*, covered herself with a veil and wrapped herself,
and sat in an open place which was on the way to Timnah;
for she saw that Shelah was grown, and she was not given to
him as a wife. . . . So she arose and went away, and laid aside
her veil and put on *the garments of her widowhood*" (Gen.
38:14, 19).

We frequently do not see how many inroads relativism
has made in our thinking. This is particularly the case in
any aesthetic judgment. But the Bible makes this kind of
aesthetic judgment all the time. Consider the example of
Abigail. When Scripture states that she was a beautiful and
intelligent woman, this means that there *is* such a thing as
beauty in women. This may seem like a "common sense"
observation, but consider how desperately our culture resists the notion of objective quality in anything involving
beauty.

But aesthetic neutrality does not exist—not even in our
wardrobes—"Then Rebekah took *the choice clothes* of her
elder son Esau, which were with her in the house, and put
them on Jacob her younger son" (Gen. 27:15). Ezekiel says,
"These were your merchants in *choice* items—in *purple
clothes*, in *embroidered garments*, in chests of multicolored
apparel, in sturdy woven cords, which were in your mar-
ketplace" (Ezek. 27:24). When Achan fell into the sin of
covetousness, part of the temptation was a garment: "When
I saw among the spoils *a beautiful Babylonian garment*, two
hundred shekels of silver, and a wedge of gold weighing
fifty shekels, I coveted them and took them. And there
they are, hidden in the earth in the midst of my tent, with

the silver under it" (Josh. 7:21). And we see that Naomi gave good advice to Ruth—"Therefore wash yourself and anoint yourself, put on *your best garment* and go down to the threshing floor; but do not make yourself known to the man until he has finished eating and drinking" (Ruth 3:3). Given this framework, we can make sense of the scriptural warnings with regard to clothing. For example, we must not make superficial judgments—"For if there should come into your assembly a man with gold rings, *in fine apparel*, and there should also come in a poor man *in filthy clothes*, and you pay attention to the one wearing the fine clothes and say to him, 'You sit here in a good place,' and say to the poor man, 'You stand there,' or, 'Sit here at my footstool'" (Jas. 2:2–3). It is the fact of qualitative differences in value which present this temptation in the first place.

But quality, according to Scripture, can also be taken to an extreme. For example, Jesus dismissed luxuriant clothing: "But what did you go out to see? A man clothed in *soft garments*? Indeed, those who wear *soft clothing* are in kings' houses" (Mt. 11:8). Herod did not compare well to the masculine look of John the Baptist. And of course preening oneself is out: "But all their works they do to be seen by men. They make their phylacteries broad and enlarge the borders of their garments" (Mt. 23:5).

In none of this may we forget that God supplies all our needs. We should trust God for our clothes—"Now if God so clothes the grass of the field, which today is, and tomorrow is thrown into the oven, will He not much more *clothe you*, O you of little faith?" (Mt. 6:30).

The point of this accumulation of passages should be obvious: *clothing matters.* Clothing reflects joy or sadness, wealth or poverty, festivity or routine activity. Given all of this, it is not surprising that God prohibits androgyny, or confusion of the sexes, in the way we dress.

> A woman shall not wear anything that pertains to a man,
> nor shall a man put on a woman's garment, for all who do so
> are an abomination to the LORD your God. (Deut. 22:5)

The Bible prohibits, in the strongest language, the kind
of sexual confusion which would result in a woman wearing a man's clothing or a man wearing a woman's clothing.
To be guilty of confusion on that point is to be guilty of an
abomination.

Unless a culture is in the grip of decadent rebellion,
clear differences exist in clothing. Just as the prohibition
of stealing presupposes private property, and the prohibition of adultery presupposes marriage, this condemnation
of androgynous dressing presupposes that men and women
dress differently. This presupposition reflects a mentality
which all Christian men should share and reflect in the way
they dress.

And, of course, we do all this, keeping in mind the sar-
torial exhortations of one of our contemporary poets, who
reminds us that "every girl's crazy 'bout a sharp dressed
man."

Hair: The Bible also teaches us more than perhaps we
wanted to know on the subject of hair and hair length. The
passage which gives us the most information on the subject
is an important one and worth quoting at length.

> Now I praise you, brethren, that you remember me in all
> things and keep the traditions just as I delivered them to
> you. But I want you to know that the head of every man is
> Christ, the head of woman is man, and the head of Christ is
> God. Every man praying or prophesying, having his head
> covered, dishonors his head. But every woman who prays or
> prophesies with her head uncovered dishonors her head, for
> that is one and the same as if her head were shaved. For if a
> woman is not covered, let her also be shorn. But if it is shame-
> ful for a woman to be shorn or shaved, let her be covered.
> For a man indeed ought not to cover his head, since he is the

image and glory of God; but woman is the glory of man. For man is not from woman, but woman from man. Nor was man created for the woman, but woman for the man. For this reason the woman ought to have a symbol of authority on her head, because of the angels. Nevertheless, neither is man independent of woman, nor woman independent of man, in the Lord. For as woman came from man, even so man also comes through woman; but all things are from God. Judge among yourselves. Is it proper for a woman to pray to God with her head uncovered? Does not even nature itself teach you that if a man has long hair, it is a dishonor to him? But if a woman has long hair, it is a glory to her; for her hair is given to her for a covering. But if anyone seems to be contentious, we have no such custom, nor *do* the churches of God. (1 Cor. 11:2–16)

In verse fourteen of this passage, Paul teaches us that distinctions of hair length between men and women are *natural*, not cultural. The fact that women are given long hair is part of God's creation order, and men are to have short hair for the same reason.

Some have taken this passage to mean that women should wear veils, but this is not in view at all. Paul says that a woman's hair is given to her for a *natural* veil (v. 15). Certainly, if a woman with a shaved head were converted, she should wear a veil until her hair grows out.

"Well, oh yeah?" we say, *quarreling with an apostle*, "how long is long? How short is short?" The answer is really very simple; nature itself can teach this lesson. Often we become logic-choppers for no other reason than that the Word of God has crossed us in what we want to do. When we see someone on the street, is it possible to describe him as having long hair or her as having short hair? Of course. When we give descriptions of others, we do this all the time.

Long and short are comparative terms. Hair is not long compared to a long, five-hundred mile trip. It is long compared to hair that is short. And Paul requires that in such comparisons that the men have short hair and the women long hair. But some might want to press it, insisting on the kind of dress code one might find at a fundamentalist Bible college. "Two-inches and shorter is considered short." But the Bible does not require that men have crewcuts. It requires that men have short hair relative to the women. In particular a man should have shorter hair than his *wife*. Nature itself teaches this to those who use their heads. A man might have hair over his ears which is very short compared to his wife's hair down her back. This passage prohibits two things: the first is role reversal in hair length with men having long hair and women having short hair; the second is androgynous blurring, where hair length is no longer relevant in making distinctions between men and women.

Although women are to have long hair, there is a sense in which the men are to be, well, hairier. The early church father, Clement of Alexandria, put it somewhat quaintly somewhere, when he said, "It is therefore impious to desecrate the symbol of manhood, hairiness." Clement was at war with the widespread practice in degenerate Rome of dipilation, or removal of hair from the body. He was at war with the rampant effeminate foppery of his day and waged that war far more consistently than do we.

While women have longer hair, which is their glory, men have been gifted with more hair. In particular, men have been given beards. My point here is not that it is a sin or wrong in any way to be clean-shaven, but that the Bible does teach that a beard is a sign of masculine honor. In a culture such as ours, when androgyny is the order of the day, we should not be surprised to find beards becoming rare, and body shavings become common. Whenever men seek to look like women, a beard mars the effect.

When David's emissaries were insulted, the king was very kind to them: "And the king said, 'Wait at Jericho until your beards have grown, and then return'" (2 Sam. 10:4–5; cf. 1 Chr. 19:5). To shave a beard was a sign of grief and distress—"Certain men came from Shechem, from Shiloh, and from Samaria, eighty men with their beards shaved and their clothes torn, having cut themselves, with offerings and incense in their hand, to bring *them* to the house of the LORD" (Jer. 41:5). Ezra responds to a calamity in the same way, "So when I heard this thing, I tore my garment and my robe, and plucked out some of the hair of my head and beard, and sat down astonished" (Ezra 9:3; *cf.* Is. 15:2).

Beards are spoken of highly. The unity of the saints is pictured as precious oil on a beard—"It is like the precious oil upon the head, running down on the beard, the beard of Aaron, running down on the edge of his garments" (Ps. 133:2).

We know that the Lord Jesus had a beard, not from any description in the New Testament, but from one of Isaiah's prophecies: "The Lord GOD has opened My ear; and I was not rebellious, nor did I turn away. I gave My back to those who struck Me, and My cheeks to those who plucked out the beard" (Is. 50: 5–6).

This all fits with a distinction which God required the Israelites to maintain between themselves and the Canaanitic peoples around them: "They shall not make any bald place on their heads, *nor shall they shave the edges of their beards* nor make any cuttings in their flesh" (Lev. 21:5); "You shall not shave around the sides of your head, nor shall you disfigure the edges of your beard" (Lev. 19:27).

This is part of the holiness code which was fulfilled in Christ (Eph. 2:14–15), so we do not say that Christian men *must* have a beard. This is an issue where Christian liberty must certainly dictate. At the same time, we should remember that God in his kindness has given men the opportunity to make sure no one mistakes their sex, and that a statement of this kind is entirely appropriate in an age like ours. While wearing a beard is not necessary, it is necessary to reject the widespread dislike of beards. Scripturally speaking, a beard is a sign of masculine honor.

Jewelry: The same kind of issues arise when we consider questions of jewelry. What are we to make of eyebrow rings and so forth? Generally, on issues like this, Christians don't have any problem going sideways, but they usually do so on the basis of some traditional value. However, the disintegration of the culture we see around us should have taught us a long time ago that our traditional values are really nothing but a mud fence built to withstand a tidal wave.

Many times Christian men just assume that their dislike of "the earring" is related to their being terminally unhip. When they see the whole culture moving in that direction, they do not feel as though they have any biblical basis for saying *no*. And if they were to say *no*, they do not know how they would justify it scripturally.

What does the Bible teach us about the very common practices of body-piercing and body mutilation? Before addressing the biblical instruction, we should begin with certain self-evident truths.

The current mania for self-mutilation and piercing is clearly a manifestation of a deep-seated pagan drive to rebel against God. We should make sure that we grant to unbelievers the dignity of explaining and demonstrating to us what it is they are doing. The widespread practice of body modification and mutilation is *a religious phenomenon of the first order of magnitude.* Anyone who maintains otherwise is simply not listening. The irony is that the many imitators of such practices that we find in the church today are simultaneously insisting that we pay close attention to what the world is doing while all the time studiously ignoring what the world is saying it all means. Piercing parlors (a minor industry has grown up around this) will, for a fee, punch a hole in your lips, eyebrows, tongues, noses, nipples, navels, or genitalia. And yet some Christians persist in saying, "But you can't really say from Scripture that such things are *necessarily* sinful." What would it take? A tattoo saying, "I love the devil"? Our situation must be understood as a cultural manifestation of an underlying loss of faith and coherence. Men and women need to *belong*. If they do not have and cherish the mark of baptism, they will eventually drive a hole in themselves and take on the insignia of rebellious servitude. Rebellion against God necessarily involves slavery to sin, slavery to lusts, slavery to folly, and slavery to men.

In Scripture, piercing clearly means subordination: "Then his master shall bring him unto the judges; he shall also bring him to the door, or unto the door post; and his master shall bore his ear through with an awl; and he shall serve him for ever" (Exod. 21:6; *cf.* Deut. 15:17). When a man was entering into slavery, he was to have his ear pierced. In addition, a particular form of bodily mutilation was expressly forbidden to Israel, "Ye shall not make any cuttings in your flesh for the dead, nor print any marks upon you: I am the Lord" (Lev. 19:28). The priests of Baal served their god in that way: "And they cried aloud, and cut themselves *after their manner* with knives and lancets, till the blood gushed out upon them" (1 Kgs. 18:28). In Proverbs 8, wisdom declares that all who hate her love death. They also love that which leads up to death—self-loathing, as evidenced by that attractive ring in the tongue.

A glib response to all this might be to say, "Well, there are lots of examples of men wearing earrings in the Bible." Israelite men used their earrings to make the golden calf (Exod. 32:1–4), the Ishmaelites wore earrings (Judg. 8:24), and men in Israel could have their ears pierced (Deut. 15:17). Overlooked in this is the fact that the Israelite men in question had either just come out of slavery or were just going into it. Body piercing is a mark of slavery. The Ishmaelites were not part of Israel and were fit for slavery.

Another glib response among Christians might be, "Well, I would never take it *that* far." But this is not to think like a Christian should. Before asking how *much* of something we should do, we must first ask *what it means*. This practice of ours is a resurgence of the mentality—

a slave mentality—which we see condemned in the Bible: "Ye are bought with a price; be not ye the servants of men" (1 Cor. 7:23).

This of course provokes the question whether subordination is necessarily evil. Of course not. A godly form of subordination exists in the world God made in the subordination of a wife to her husband. This is why it is fully appropriate for a godly woman to have earrings (Ezek. 16:12) or culture permitting, nose rings (Gen. 24:30; Ezek.16:12; Exod. 35:22). But restraint is placed upon us even here, for Christian women are free women, submitting only to their husbands, so they should not drape themselves in chains. Their point in jewelry should be to seek to make themselves attractive to their husbands and to do so with all modesty (1 Tim. 2:8–10). However, the point of body-piercing is not to be attractive but rather the reverse. The intent is to be repulsive. A girl who wears a dog collar is saying what she thinks of herself. We do not have to agree with her point to understand it.

Working Man

Many Christian men do not think of their work, their business, their money, as being under the *specific* authority of God. We acknowledge that He owns it all, but we frequently assume that He is some kind of an absentee landlord, who doesn't much mind what we do with our business and money on a day-to-day basis. But this is clearly false.

A husband who seeks to be a godly provider must begin at the biblical beginning—"Keep your heart with all diligence, for out of it spring the issues of life" (Prov. 4:23). A man must watch his heart—it affects both business and finances. The fear of God is the beginning of knowledge in this area too—"The fear of the Lord is the beginning of knowledge, but fools despise wisdom and instruction" (Prov. 1:7).

A federal husband must serve God as he earns bread for his household, and he must do it the *way* God says—

"Through wisdom a house is built, and by understanding it is established; *by knowledge* the rooms are filled with all precious and pleasant riches" (Prov. 24:3–4). A husband must never seek to detach his service of God and his provision for his household— "By humility and the fear of the Lord are riches and honor and life" (Prov. 22:4). This process obviously begins as we seek God's blessing by means of the tithe—"Honor the Lord with your possessions, and with the firstfruits of all your increase; so your barns will be filled with plenty, and your vats will overflow with new wine" (Prov. 3:9–10). We have been trained to chant all together, "Oh, but that's in the Old Testament!" Many Christians assume that in the New Covenant we have been freed to become ingrates. But God still loves to bless those who love to bless. While we do not give to Him in order to get, we do give to get *in order to give again.*

Things Greater Than Wealth: We should also seek the blessing of God in a diligent pursuit of wisdom—"Riches and honor are with me, enduring riches and righteousness. My fruit is better than gold, yes, than fine gold, and my revenue than choice silver. I traverse the way of righteousness, in the midst of the paths of justice, that I may cause those who love me to inherit wealth, that I may fill their treasuries" (Prov. 8:18–21). Wisdom personified is speaking in this chapter, and with her presence we see a great financial blessing. But to understand the financial implications of this invitation is neither crass nor mercenary.

When someone undertakes to make a living, the first creaturely thing to do is *not* to get money. It is to *get wisdom.* Does this man know what he is doing and why? Does he know how God would have him pursue his vocational calling? Wisdom is not evidenced so much in *where* a man works but in *how* he works. Wisdom consists of more than knowing; it consists of knowing what to do with the knowledge. A wise husband seeks for wisdom as though it were gold.

A diligent provider will also seek the blessing of God through his generosity—"There is one who scatters, yet increases more; and there is one who withholds more than is right, but it leads to poverty. The generous soul will be made rich, and he who waters will also be watered himself. The people will curse him who withholds grain, but blessing will be on the head of him who sells it" (Prov. 11:24–26). John Bunyan's comment is *appropos*—"there was a man, some thought him mad, the more he gave, the more he had." God not only blesses when we give to Him; He blesses when we give to the poor. "He who has a generous eye will be blessed, for he gives of his bread to the poor" (Prov. 22:9). "He who gives to the poor will not lack, but he who hides his eyes will have many curses" (Prov. 28:27). "He who has pity on the poor lends to the Lord, and He will pay back what he has given" (Prov. 19:17).

The head of the home must establish a godly set of priorities. Although wealth is a blessing, it is by no means the *highest* blessing which God can bestow. As a man sets his priorities for business, a number of things should be in line ahead of profit.

We all know what is meant when the cliche is invoked—setting priorities means "more quality time with the kids." But too often we just invoke the phrase as though it were a mantra and the content of our priorities just assumed (which means they are picked up from the culture around us). *By what standard* must we set our priorities when it comes to the question of wealth? The Bible tells us. What is *better than* wealth? What should we *rather have* than great riches? Again, the Bible tells us. When we consider such passages, we may be surprised that the antithesis is not, for example, between wealth and family.

The Bible also teaches us to prefer reputation to wealth: "A good name is to be chosen rather than great riches, loving favor rather than silver and gold. The rich and the poor have this in common, the Lord is the maker of them all" (Prov. 22:1–2). A good name is especially important in the world of work. What constitutes a good name in business? Work managed with wisdom; work conducted with absolute honesty in fact; work done with absolute honesty in appearance; hard work; work completed on time; not taking advantage in work done for brothers; work which does not depend upon a "scheme"; work which understands propriety.

The loss of a good name is hard to repair. The fact that a man might lose his reputation is not "unfair" but rather one of the ordinary costs of doing business. People recommend businesses—or not—*all the time*. This is as it should be.

We are also told to prefer contentment to wealth: "Remove falsehood and lies far from me; give me neither poverty nor riches. Feed me with the food allotted to me; lest I be full and deny You, and say, 'Who is the Lord?' Or lest I be poor and steal, and profane the name of my God" (Prov. 30:8–9). Fundamentally, this is a prayer for *contentment*: "Lord, please give me a portion suited for me. If I get more than that I will be tempted one way. If I get less than that, I will be tempted in another." It may sound odd, but many Christians have not learned contentment with their blessings.

Humility is better than riches—"Better to be of a humble spirit with the lowly, than to divide the spoil with the proud" (Prov. 16:19). Pride is often thought to be the badge of the wealthy, but according to the Bible, it is their shame.

The Bible also praises calmness, quietness, and love over material abundance: "Better is a dry morsel with quietness, than a house full of feasting with strife" (Prov. 17:1). Better to have a bowl of cold cereal with calm surroundings than to have the Thanksgiving ham with tumult: "Better is a little with the fear of the Lord, than great treasure with trouble. Better is a dinner of herbs where love is, than a fatted calf with hatred" (Prov. 15:16–17). In this place, the fear of the Lord is equated with love, and their absence cannot be compensated with money. As a man structures his pursuit of his business, he must remember this.

Sensuality: Many men fritter away what belongs to their households because they set the pattern of stumbling into sensuality. We may be induced to throw our money away in any number of ways. As Christians we know that all sins are bad. This is obvious, but many of our sins are also *expensive.*

Consider the matter of the appetites generally: "The righteous eats to the satisfying of his soul, but the stomach of the wicked shall be in want" (Prov. 13:25). Both the righteous and the wicked have a stomach and an appetite. But the righteous can eat and be satisfied, while the wicked are driven by an appetite which is out of control. In any of the areas considered here, the issue is generally not the thing being considered, i.e. sleep, sex, etc., but rather whether or not God's law is honored, and whether or not self-control is in evidence.

Luxurious living consumes wealth and is inappropriate for the kind of man attracted to it, that is to say, a fool— "Luxury is not fitting for a fool, much less for a servant to rule over princes" (Prov. 19:10). Luxurious display is inappropriate for a fool—a fool shouldn't have it. And if he does get it, he won't have it for long. The fool thinks, *If only . . . :* "If only I could get a nice car, if only I could get those expensive clothes, if only I could get that wonderful food." But it is not fitting. The Bible condemns the wasteful use of our resources on frivolity.

> He who tills his land will have plenty of bread, but he who follows frivolity will have poverty enough! A faithful man will abound with blessings, but he who hastens to be rich will not go unpunished. To show partiality is not good, because for a piece of bread a man will transgress. A man with an evil eye hastens after riches, and does not consider that poverty will come upon him. (Prov. 28:19–22)

A number of issues are addressed in this passage—
trying to get rich quickly, showing favoritism, miserliness—
but the warning presented first is against *frivolity*. The
Hebrew word can mean either frivolity and vanity, or frivo-
lous and empty fellows. The contrast is with one who tills
his land, so the meaning is apparently referring to one who
follows vain and pleasurable pursuits instead of working.
What he follows may have the appearance of work or not,
but it still comes up empty.

A Christian man must reject sensualism—"Do not let
your heart envy sinners, but be zealous for the fear of the
Lord all the day; for surely there is a hereafter, and your
hope will not be cut off. Hear, my son, and be wise; and
guide your heart in the way. Do not mix with winebibbers,
or with gluttonous eaters of meat; for the drunkard and the
glutton will come to poverty, and drowsiness will clothe a
man with rags" (Prov. 23:17–21). Gluttony in Scripture
does *not* refer to someone having a second helping of the
mashed potatoes. Rather it refers to the sensualist—the
drunkard of food. Scripturally, the glutton is a "riotous
eater." For an example of this, the ancient Romans had a
vomitoria where guests could prepare for the "second
course." This sensual pursuit of food leads to poverty.

"He who loves pleasure will be a poor man; he who
loves wine and oil will not be rich" (Prov. 21:17). The issue is not the pleasure but rather the inordinate love of it.
Whatever the foolish man loves (in this case, sensual expe-
rience), he winds up losing—"There is desirable treasure,
and oil in the dwelling of the wise, but a foolish man squan-
ders it" (Prov. 21:20).

Laziness: A lazy man is not necessarily apathetic; he
may have a great intensity of desire—"The desire of the
lazy man kills him, for his hands refuse to labor. He covets
greedily all day long, but the righteous gives and does not
spare" (Prov. 21:25–26).

When we come to consider laziness, we will find no

real help in looking at the Hebrew word for *lazy man* or *sluggard*. It means . . . simply *lazy man* or *sluggard*. Some things are so universal that they translate well into any language; we all understand what a shirker is.

But however common it is, the Bible teaches that laziness remains a disgrace—"He who has a slack hand becomes poor, but the hand of the diligent makes rich. He who gathers in summer is a wise son; he who sleeps in harvest is a son who causes shame" (Prov. 10:4–5). As a sin which brings shame, we should consider well some of its identifying characteristics. As we learn, we should remember that laziness has an obvious alternative: "Go to the ant, you sluggard!" (Prov. 6:6–11). The alternative is working hard.

Laziness has no follow through. A lazy man may have bursts of activity, and he may even get something done during one of them. But he does not maintain; he does not persevere—"The lazy man does not roast what he took in hunting, but diligence is man's precious possession" (Prov. 12:27). Sometimes the lack of follow-through is extraordinary—a very simple thing could be done to bring a project to completion, but he does not do it: "A lazy man buries his hand in the bowl, and will not so much as bring it to his mouth again. Strike a scoffer, and the simple will become wary; rebuke one who has understanding, and he will discern knowledge" (Prov. 19:24–25). The solution to laziness is seen in this passage as well—the lazy must be permitted to eat their own cooking.

Those who resolve to let the lazy face the consequences had better be deaf, because laziness is full of excuses: "The lazy man says, 'There is a lion outside! I shall be slain in the streets!'" (Prov. 22:13). Sometimes the excuses are unreasonable—the ancient Hebrew equivalent of "the dog ate my homework" or "aliens kidnapped me . . . what year is it?" Other times the excuses may seem more reasonable, but *the results are still the same*—"The lazy man will not plow because of winter; he will beg during harvest and have nothing" (Prov. 20:4). Whether the work did not get done because of aliens or because of a flat tire, the results are the same—the work is not done.

Laziness is full of "wisdom": "In all labor there is profit, but idle chatter leads only to poverty. The crown of the wise is their riches, but the foolishness of fools is folly" (Prov. 14:23–24). The lazy man wears his foolish talk like a crown, the counterpoint to the wealth which crowns a wise man. The lazy man may be full of proverbial wisdom concerning work, but his wisdom is like the legs of a lame man (Prov. 26:7). Consider: "The lazy man is wiser in his own eyes than seven men who can answer sensibly" (Prov. 26:16). Even though his lifestyle is ludicrous and the folly is apparent to everyone but the social worker, the lazy man has it all figured out. He has more wisdom (in his own eyes) than seven wise men.

Laziness is an irritation to others and is necessarily a grief to those who are dependent upon the one who lets them down—"As vinegar to the teeth and smoke to the eyes, so is the lazy man to those who send him" (Prov. 10:26). This is not surprising. If one of them is lazy, two men will have very different ideas of what constitutes diligence.

The Word teaches us that laziness compounds with interest—"Laziness casts one into a deep sleep, and an idle person will suffer hunger" (Prov. 19:15); "The soul of a lazy man desires, and has nothing; but the soul of the diligent shall be made rich" (Prov. 13:4). Laziness is not rest; it does not prepare for work. It only prepares for more laziness. As the laziness grows, so does frustrated desire.

When a man observes the sabbath, he is prepared and refreshed for his work. But when he has "rested" for several months, he is incapacitated for work. The way out is not more rest but rather repentance.

Laziness also provokes hastiness and deceit—"The plans of the diligent lead surely to plenty, but those of everyone who is hasty, surely to poverty. Getting treasures by a lying tongue is the fleeting fantasy of those who seek death" (Prov.

21:5–6). Diligence, the opposite of laziness, is here contrasted with hastiness and lies. A refusal of all due diligence is a setup for boneheadedness and lies.

Of course, laziness is hard—"The way of the lazy man is like a hedge of thorns, but the way of the upright is a highway" (Prov. 15:19). Proverbs teaches us that laziness is counterproductive; *it does not accomplish its desired end*— "The hand of the diligent will rule, but the lazy man will be put to forced labor" (Prov. 12:24).

All things considered, laziness is an object lesson—"I went by the field of the lazy man, and by the vineyard of the man devoid of understanding" (Prov. 24:30). When lazy men marry, and they do, the consequences of the sin spread to others. The object lesson should be taken to heart long before a man even thinks about taking a wife.

The only alternative is honest work, with emphasis placed on the word *honest*. The problem of dishonesty in work and labor is a difficult one to address because it is often the case that the first one "lied to" is the liar himself. He is dishonest in his work and labor, and in order to do this most effectively, he must be dishonest first with himself. Remember that the truth about oneself is not seen by looking into the heart; the truth is found by looking into *the mirror of the Word* (Jas. 1:24–25). The Word of God is the only solution to self-deception.

A man who wants his household to belong to the Lord must support that household with work that belongs to Him. And the only kind of work that belongs to God is honest work—"Honest weights and scales are the Lord's; *all the weights in the bag are His work*" (Prov. 16:11). The Lord *identifies* with honest work. The weights in the bag are His, the nails in the wall are His, the repair job is His, the bookkeeping work is His—provided it is done honestly.

An honest man must learn not to procrastinate with regard to his obligations—"Do not withhold good from those to whom it is due, when it is in the power of your hand to do so. Do not say to your neighbor, 'Go, and come back, and tomorrow I will give it,' when you have it with you" (Prov. 3:27–28). A man must deal with his responsibilities in order. An important application of this principle is to pay *oldest bills first*.

Financial Entanglements: A wise man avoids financial entanglements. The author of Proverbs clearly had strong feelings about co-signing notes and related entanglements— "He who is surety for a stranger will suffer, but one who hates being surety is secure" (Prov. 11:15; 6:1–5). "A man devoid of understanding shakes hands in a pledge, and becomes surety for his friend" (Prov. 17:18). More people get in financial trouble *with their friends* than with complete strangers—"Do not be one of those who shakes hands in a pledge, one of those who is surety for debts; if you have nothing with which to pay, why should he take away your bed from under you?" (Prov. 22:26–27).

One popular form of financial entanglement is that of debt. More Christian men have ruined their households through debt than any other financial foolishness—"The rich rules over the poor, and the borrower is servant to the lender" (Prov. 22:7). If a man wants his wife to be a free woman and wants his children to grow up free, then saddling them with debt is not the scriptural way to do it.

Some men have sought to provide for the future of their household through various "get-rich-quick" schemes. But the Bible tells us what happens to money which comes in this way—"An inheritance gained hastily at the beginning will not be blessed at the end" (Prov. 20:21). This may be honestly gained, but it still will be difficult to honestly *retain*. Speed also puts a dent in honesty, and as we have seen, dishonesty is a loser—"Wealth gained by dishonesty will be diminished, but he who gathers by labor will increase" (Prov. 13:11). Another "fast track" to wealth is through the foolishness of others, but the Lord is not pleased— "One who increases his possessions by usury and extortion gathers it for him who will pity the poor" (Prov. 28:8).

A man must also be conservative and very cautious about his financial dealings. A husband and father has a duty to save—"A good man leaves an inheritance to his children's children, but the wealth of the sinner is stored up for the righteous" (Prov. 13:22). The bumpersticker which proclaims how the inhabitants of the motor home are spending their children's inheritance is godless folly. At the same time, children, particularly indolent children, must not be presumptuous. The inheritance should not be dispersed without careful thought—"A wise servant will rule over a son who causes shame, and will share an inheritance among the brothers" (Prov. 17:2).

A man must never forget the Lord who gives wealth— "Riches do not profit in the day of wrath, but righteousness delivers from death" (Prov. 11:4); "The curse of the Lord is on the house of the wicked, but He blesses the home of the just" (Prov. 3:33); "Treasures of wickedness profit nothing, but righteousness delivers from death" (Prov. 10:2); "Good understanding gains favor, but the way of the unfaithful is hard" (Prov. 13:15). And it ought to be.

Federal Husband and Society

Masculinity and Cultural Hierarchy

Peter's teaching that men should live considerately with their wives as with a "weaker vessel" has contributed to more than one lively discussion between men and women. What exactly did he mean by that? In that passage, he says this, "Husbands, likewise, dwell with them with understanding, giving honor to the wife, as to the weaker vessel, and as being heirs together of the grace of life, that your prayers may not be hindered" (1 Pet. 3:7).

We should begin by noting that *whatever* Peter intended here is to be received by Christians as the Word of God, and with no back chat. However, this is not the same thing as having to submit to interpretive distortions or misunderstandings of the passage. And there are such misunderstandings.

The most obvious distortion to reject is that of feminist egalitarianism within the church, which wants to escape the plain force of the words. But Peter's words really leave no room for maneuvering. Husbands are told to honor their wives and to live considerately with them, treating them as weaker vessels. Fortunately, most believers understand that overt feminism and biblical Christianity are incompatible, and they have little difficulty resisting any distortion of Peter's teaching in this direction.

But a second distortion is quite another matter and presents a forceful temptation to conservative believers. This is the distortion that we may call masculinist egalitarianism. This view holds that men are in one category and women in another, and any given member of one category bears the same relationship to any given member of the other. In other words, it assumes that men are the leaders of women and that women are weaker than men. The resultant view of society is that "men are in charge." This is true enough, but it goes nowhere. In charge of what? Men as men are in charge of nothing, and women as women are in submission to nothing.

In this masculinist view, the assumption of the authority of men over women can clearly be seen. But the egalitarian emphasis should also be clear. Because, as the thinking goes, any man can lead any woman, consequently any given marriage, any family, is on the same fundamental level as any other family.

But human society as created by God is hierarchical—"Blessed are you, O land, when your king is the son of nobles" (Eccl. 10:17). Despite an unremitting stream of agitated egalitarian rhetoric since the time of the French Revolution, all societies still contain both men and women who are distributively educated and uneducated, intelligent and unintelligent, refined and unrefined, upper and lower class, etc. The constant din of propaganda means that we are hesitant to affirm that this is so, but "facts is facts and facts will out." This means that an accurate picture of society will show both men and women in the educated classes, and both men and women in the uneducated classes. Both sexes show up converted and unconverted, polished and unpolished, intelligent and unintelligent, tall and short, fat and thin. A biblical view of culture consequently requires a nobility of some sort.

The masculinist egalitarian tends to assume that the broader relationship between men and women is foremost, with other social factors being nonexistent or negligible.

Because of this assumption of the primacy of men *generally* over women *generally*, the adherent of this view assumes that every male should be prepared to lead any home and that every female should be prepared to step into any marriage ready to follow. He also necessarily assumes that the resultant families are roughly equal in ability, status, etc. This has the impact which egalitarianism always has. Because women of ability in this view are considered with grave suspicion to be closet feminists, some action must be taken to retard or restrict the abilities of such women.

In the hierarchical and biblical view, the relationship of women to men is *first familial*, and then as a consequence, a larger (and very complex) cultural and societal relationship between the sexes emerges. This means that wives are to submit to, and provide help to, their own husbands (and no one else). As a result of this submission in countless families, a larger patriarchal society will in fact emerge. However, this patriarchal society will necessarily contain a number of women who are far more intelligent, educated, and "stronger" than numerous individual men. No society is truly patriarchal unless it contains a significant number of noble women, "stronger" in many ways than a number of the men.

But for the masculinist egalitarian, a highly educated noble woman is considered a threat to "men," and as someone who is being uppity—someone who resists Peter's teaching about the weaker vessel. But whose weaker vessel is she? The biblical answer is, her husband's. She is not society's weaker vessel, and she is not Joe-on-the-street's weaker vessel.

A simplistic, traditionalist "family values" position says that men are leaders and women are followers. It would be more accurate to say that husbands are heads and their wives are their helpers. Because some of the men are leaders and others are followers, their respective wives will be helping them lead, or helping them follow, or helping them at every

conceivable stage in between. Such an understanding preserves both the biblical understanding of headship and
submission in the home and the biblical understanding of a
culture.

This complex relationship is illustrated in the divine
requirements for the government of the church. Paul flatly
excludes any woman, no matter how gifted, from holding
"authority over a man" in the church of Christ—"Let a
woman learn in silence with all submission. And I do not
permit a woman to teach or to have authority over a man,
but to be in silence. For Adam was formed first, then Eve.
And Adam was not deceived, but the woman being deceived,
fell into transgression. Nevertheless she will be saved in
childbearing if they continue in faith, love, and holiness,
with self-control" (1 Tim. 2:11–15). Clearly, women may
not be elders or ministers of the word. No matter how
much modern exegetes huff and puff, they cannot blow the
verse down.

At the same time, Paul assumes that a bishop will be
married and will rule his household well (1 Tim. 3: 2, 5). If
this is considered thoughtfully for a moment, this clearly
means that his wife will have considerable influence in the
church through her influence on her husband. The same
pattern is seen in every trans-family cultural setting.
Through submission to their husbands, some women can
have far more influence in a culture or subculture than some
of the men do. This is very good; this is the strength of the
weaker vessel.

The masculinist problem is that of seeing women generally having to submit to men generally. In contrast, the
biblical pattern is that particular women are to be in submission to particular fathers and husbands. This prevents
their submission to other men, which, considering some of
the men out there, is a good thing. This means a particular
noble woman could in many respects be the superior of a
particular man. She would not be *his* weaker vessel. This
would be an excellent reason for her not to marry such a

man—from that point on, Scripture would require her to be a respectful and dutiful wife to him. A man of lesser abilities is able to be a biblical head to some women but not to all. A woman of greater ability is able to submit joyfully to some men, but not to all. Understanding this will take us back to the biblical pattern of complex hierarchy in society and also bring us to reject the simplistic hierarchy of "Me, Tarzan; You, Any Given Female."

C.S. Lewis once commented on this pattern as he contrasted the station of a very great woman (who was a submissive wife) and the station of a common man:

> But I should feel sorry for the common man, such as myself, who was led by this speech into the egregious mistake of walking into Belmont and behaving as though Portia really were an unlessoned girl. A man's forehead reddens to think of it. She may speak thus to Bassanio: but we had better remember that we are dealing with a great lady.

Anyone familiar with the writing of Lewis knows how much he detested feminism, but this passage shows that he also was embarrassed by the kind of men who think more highly of themselves than they ought. He recognized that God had made a world hostile to -*isms* and friendly to humility.

Now an elder of a Christian church, who is committed to one woman, as Paul says, will soon find that his wife has a great deal of influence in the church—more perhaps than many of the individual men in the church. Does this open the door for pushy preachers' and elders' wives to become *de facto* 'eldettes'? Does this create an opportunity for those who are advancing the feminist agenda in the church? Not at all.

The first point to be made is that this hierarchical pattern is not really conjectural. An elder who is married and has the kind of helper he must have if he is managing his household as Scripture requires, will be a far more effective elder because of the influence of his wife on him. The help he is to receive from his wife is not limited to bearing his children and preparing his meals. At the same time, her influence on the church is indirect and is wielded through her ministry to him. As an individual, the wife of a pastor holds no office in the church. As a submissive wife, she is likely her husband's closest friend, confidant, counselor, and advisor.

Esther, a submissive wife, had more influence than all the elders of Israel. Given the nature of this influence, no scriptural fault can be found with it. Mordecai was even prepared to blame her if she tried to get away from the influence she could wield through submission. In a similar submissive way, a godly pastor's wife will be a tremendous blessing in the church. "How do you think James is doing? Do you think you should give him a call?"

The second point to make is that truth can always be distorted, and until the resurrection, it always will be. When those who distort it are pushy women, it can be distorted in remarkably destructive ways. Scripture does not establish a separate office called "married to an elder," which gives the bearer the right to be offended if anything in the church does not go her way. Certainly, no woman may have any personal authority in the government of the church. And certainly, an unsubmissive woman may grab and run off with any comments here indicating that some women must have influence in the church. But she could also justify her behavior by pointing out the unbiblical behavior of reactionary males, who cannot defend their doctrine of blanket male superiority from Scripture and whose only defense for their behavior is that feminism is unscriptural and that their position is "not feminism."

The real issue is whether or not a particular teaching is true. If it is true, this will certainly not prevent distortions. After all, Peter tells us that ignorant and unstable people twisted Paul's writings—as difficult to understand as they were. Paul himself tells us people mangled his words but went on to add that their condemnation was just. The question is therefore not, "What could so-and-so do with this?" but rather, "Is it scriptural? Is it *right*?" If those women who want to run the show can get around the Scripture, they can also get around anything else.

My objection is that the masculinist position is just as unbiblical as the feminist position. Men who are not leaders in the home, where Scripture requires it, are commonly tempted to make up for this abdication elsewhere. This is sometimes found in the comfort of knowing that "men" have it over "women." But this is no-cost authority. A generally diffused masculinist bluster is no substitute for the godly authority which flows from consistent Christ-like service in the home. Such bluster is common among masculinists, but genuine masculine authority is often far absent.

In the final analysis, the problem of women who overstep their bounds in a church is not their problem. The difficulty is with the men who let them.

Masculine Security

Balance is very difficult to achieve. We cannot deal with the errors of feminism without some men overreacting and maintaining that all women should be barefoot, etc.

For example, in conservative Christian circles, a number of men have become concerned about ladies' Bible studies or fellowships because of the potential damage that can be done to the home. For example, what happens when women studying their Bibles get ahead of their husbands spiritually? For some reason, people always assume that the solution is to slow the women down rather than to speed the men up.

The questions are not just limited to the study of the Scriptures. I have often been asked, "What is the purpose of having women get a rigorous liberal arts college education?" And following the logic, what is the purpose behind having them get a formal education at all?

When men ask about the roles of women in a culture of

Christians who seek to recover the biblical balance, multitudes of practical questions arise. "Should she do this . . . or that?" If, as I argue later, women should not be involved in combat, then perhaps we should go back and question everything that modern women do. Should a woman go to college? Should a woman study the Scriptures?

We must distinguish between an activity and purpose for an activity. The first answers the question, *What is she doing?* and the second, *Why is she doing it?* While a general pattern can be identified between activities and their purpose, this cannot necessarily be done in a one-to-one correspondence.

The Bible teaches that a woman's fundamental orientation is to be domestic. As we have seen, multiple passages show this (e.g., Tit. 2:1–5; Prov. 31:10–31; 1 Tim. 2:15; 5:3–14). For many, this makes the question a very simple one. Women should therefore limit themselves to activities which are overtly and obviously domestic—e.g., pots and pans. But one person's engagement in a particular activity can be completely different in motivation and direction than another person's participation in that same activity. When a Christian woman is asked *what* she is doing, her answer may be exactly what some pagan feminist might answer. "I'm studying for a physics test. Why?" But when a Christian woman is asked *why* she is doing what she is doing, her answer must radically diverge from any answer which an unbeliever could give. Her answer, in other words, should be oriented to the home. "I am studying physics in order to glorify God through being a godly and effective wife and mother." In other words, she must relate her activity to the scripturally-assigned purpose for that activity. If, for example, she is a younger married woman, she is responsible to integrate what she does with what Paul assigns as the general duties of younger married women.

In the meantime, this potential flexibility in this response distresses some traditionalist males, who do not want a women doing anything more than fifteen feet from Home

Economics 101. Consequently, we hear the response, "But *that* can't help you be a wife and mother!" The woman should understand that *that* depends upon whom she marries and what kind of mother she wants to be. In 1903, J. Gresham Machen's mom published *The Bible in Browning.* She was quite an accomplished woman. She read widely, including the New Testament in Greek, English and French classics. And what was her vocation? Mother.

As with everything else, we should turn to Scripture to determine what activities are consistent with a woman's domestic calling. Some of the things which we should consider would be correcting a man's theology (Acts 18:26); writing Scripture (Lk. 1:46–55; 1 Sam. 2:1–10); buying real estate (Prov. 31:16); judging a nation (Judg. 4:4–5); leading armies (Judg. 4:14); assassination (Judg. 5:24–25); hand-delivering the book of Romans (Rom. 16:1–2); and laboring evangelistically alongside men (Phil. 4:3). Men who are secure in a biblical definition of masculinity and femininity will not be threatened when they meet women who conform to that biblical description.

Neither is the Bible silent on those things which are inconsistent with a woman's domestic calling. They would include formal exposition of Scripture to men (1 Tim. 2:12), serving as an elder in a Christian church (1 Tim. 2:12), or leading a husband (Eph. 5:24).

As for Me and My House

Famous phrases have a way of falling into the nether regions of our minds. We think we know them because we have heard them so often, but we really do not. Rather than true scriptural knowledge, such phrases usually just lull us to sleep. One such phrase is "As for me and my house":

> Now therefore, fear the Lord, serve Him in sincerity and in truth, and put away the gods which your fathers served on the other side of the River and in Egypt. Serve the Lord! And if it seems evil to you to serve the Lord, choose for

yourselves this day whom you will serve, whether the gods which your fathers served that were on the other side of the River, or the gods of the Amorites, in whose land you dwell. But as for me and my house, we will serve the Lord. (Josh. 24:14–15)

Joshua is speaking to the people at the ceremony of covenant renewal at Shechem. We need to pay attention both to the context of his exhortation and to the content of it. Many misunderstand covenant renewal because they misunderstand forgiveness of sin. God in His mercy picks us up where we are and not where we should have been. The effects of sin are so profound and so pervasive that sinners who fall away from God's covenant can never find their *own* way back again. After two centuries of disobedience, our people can not even gather up the pieces, much less reassemble them. The same principle applied to God's people in the Old Testament.

First, the context: Joshua has gathered the people and has reviewed for them the history of their nation, beginning with the idolatry of Abraham's people. He talks about the deliverance of Abraham and his family and goes over the redemption of the Israelite people from Egypt. He mentions how the Lord had cared for them in the wilderness, and how the Lord fought for them as they began the conquest of Canaan. This rehearsal of their history, including the times of their disobedience and sins, is the basis of his exhortation in verses 14–15. He charges them to put away their idols, two kinds of idols.

They are to put away the idols they had in *Egypt* before the Lord redeemed them, brought them out, and established His covenant with them at Sinai. They were charged to put away the idols they had retained from their pre-Christian past.

Joshua, also, tells them to put away the idols their fathers served *on the other side of the River*—the Jordan. Notice that these gods were gods that came into Israel *after* their great redemption from Egypt. In short, both kinds of gods must be put away—whether gods of the antithesis or gods of synthesis.

The content of his exhortation here is simple and brief. *Fear* the Lord. *Serve* the Lord. Fear and serve Him in *sincerity* and *truth*. Put away all other gods. Joshua then sets before the people a stirring example. He does not know what course others may take, but as for him, he will serve the Lord, and his house with him.

Our culture swarms with little gods like the frogs of Egypt. But the gods of Egypt do have the advantage of being relatively easy to identify. They are the gods of antithesis—Satan-worship, blasphemy, rank atheism, and so forth.

Synthetic Gods: The gods of synthesis, the gods of gray and off-white, the gods which sidle up next to a man in order to whisper devotional encouragements to him, are all together something else. These lords of compromise, these gods of soft counsel, *are dangerous.* Because of them the modern church is languishing, and the church is languishing because the households in Israel—and I am including the households this book comes to—must tear down some idols. These gods of synthesis are just as much a part of the antithesis as the others, but are far more dangerous because they are harder to see.

Let me mention a few of these spiritual pests. First of these is another god under the *name* Jehovah. Aaron sought to have the people serve the Lord, while hoping the golden calf would not be too much of a distraction, and who knows, perhaps to some poor unlettered Israelite such a concrete representation of Jehovah might even provide some kind of spiritual help. This is a free country, and there is no legal restriction prohibiting a man from calling that pathetic little idol in his mind . . . Jesus. There is no reason his tiny god can't be called Jehovah, Lord of Hosts, God of Battles. Of course, having considered the attributes of such a god, he usually doesn't.

Another such god is the god of the republicans and an

occasional renegade democrat—the god of civic religion and prayer breakfasts. This god would have been happily served by a pragmatic pagan like Cicero. This is the god to whom some want to offer prayer in the government schools. Such prayers would not get past the little two-foot space right above the acoustic tiles in most classrooms, which is just fine, because that is where this god lives.

Another is the god of personal peace and prosperity. He is the god of savings accounts, pensions, and insurance plans. The apostle Paul tells us in Ephesians that greed is idolatry. Christians have heard, many times, the assurance that material blessings are consistent with Christianity. *This is quite true*, but we must never forget the potential this blessing has to consume devotion to Christ. This wonderful statement, "as for me and my house," is not an inspirational quote to be matted and framed. It must be lived.

Many modern men are not up to this. The men of our generation have had a failure of nerve. They have abdicated their responsibilities. Few can deny that we are in the midst of a crisis of leadership. To use the biblical term, we have fallen into the sin of rank unbelief. God has always promised tremendous blessings for those who keep His covenant faithfully. But we, wise in our own conceits, no longer believe Him. We have fallen so far away from His Word that we no longer know what a covenant is. Consequently, we do not understand the world around us.

Social Covenants: Until we return to the covenant, we have no way of comprehending the cultural chaos which surrounds us. The clamor of modernity staggers from one crisis to the next. How is it that we have come to be ruled by such foolishness? In order to answer this question, we must not heal the wound lightly. Given the extent of our crisis, the temptation is constant to dab around the edges of the wound—it hurts too much to do anything else.

God always deals with men by means of covenant. He is a covenant-making and covenant-keeping God. This sounds nice and very religious, but what does it mean? As covered earlier in the book, these covenants are a solemn bond, sovereignly administered, with attendant blessings and curses. To review, God made a covenant of creation with Adam before the fall (Hos. 6:7); when we all sinned in Adam, He made a covenant of redemption with Adam (Gen. 3:15), Noah (Gen. 6:17–22; 8:20–22; 9:1–7; 9:8–17), Abraham (Gen. 17:1–2), Moses (Exod. 2:24), and David (2 Sam. 7:12–16). These latter covenants were not a series of disconnected and unrelated covenants, as though God were changing His mind every few centuries about what He was to do with men. These are all part of the one great unfolding covenant of grace, which finds its final great fulfillment in the passion and work of the Lord Jesus Christ (Heb. 8:7–12).

Just as the Lord deals with mankind through covenants, He created us in such a way that we also must deal with one another under Him by means of covenants. At the center of our lives, we find that such covenants are *inescapable*. We cannot function without them because they are woven into our bones. The covenants in this category are those of marriage (Mal. 3:14–15), the institution of the church (Lk. 22:20), and the civil order (Rom. 13:1–7). By ignoring God's instructions on these covenants, we may become covenantally confused and disobedient. We do *not* become uncovenantal. We are either keeping our covenants, or we are breaking them.

These three covenant institutions have been established among us directly by the hand of God. We have no more authority to alter or abolish them to suit our tastes or liking than we have the right to repeal gravity. But it is not enough for Christians to acknowledge the existence of these covenant realities; we must also correctly understand their relationship to one another. It would be a serious mistake to line them up in a row of three and then merely assign respective biblical duties to each. Each covenant institution certainly does have its respective duties, but we must first understand that the covenanted institutions of church and civil society are made up of covenanted family units.

Each family has certain assigned duties within its own sphere—education, health care, and so forth. But together families also contribute a molecular strength in the makeup of the two other trans-family governments, which are civil order and the church. Each family makes this contribution for blessing when it is offered in understanding belief, and it is received by the two broader covenant communities in the same faith.

Civil Questions: Because of the crisis of masculinity in our homes, that representation is not being offered by our households, and if it were offered, it would be received by our civil order only with laughter and by an ignorant theological indignation in our churches. In short, we are in high rebellion against God's design for family and culture. With regard to our understanding of the family, we have fallen away. We in the church like to disguise that rebellion by talking about family values a lot. This family values talk amounts to nothing more than an eager desire for more G-rated movies or a more efficient nursery at church. We *never* talk about familial representation in the church or familial authority in the civil realm.

Our men have become spiritual eunuchs. At the head and heart of each family is a man. He cannot help being biologically male, but disobedience can certainly turn him away from being masculine, i.e., that masculinity which embraces headship, takes the initiative, serves responsibly, provides for his own, and represents his household to the other governments established by God. Modern Christian men can be divided into two categories—those who have acquiesced to the current dictates requiring this effeminacy and those who think they have not capitulated because they are still allowed to beat their chests at home. Those in the latter category must come to realize their broader cultural impotence. What does leadership in the household actually mean? That the man gets to hold the remote when the family watches television? That he gets to park the car when the family goes to church? What it really means is that he has the responsibility before God to wake up.

When our Supreme Court made its infamous decision to allow the slaughter of infants, the Christians of our nation were so covenantally blind that we did not see it for what it was—the abortion of the covenanted family. This is not to minimize in any way the horrific nature of the abortion carnage itself; God is just and He will judge. But why did we not even see the other problem? Consider the result of that decision. When a woman is considering an abortion, the Court informed us that this is a decision between her and her doctor. As far as our civil order is concerned, whether she is married or not is completely irrelevant. *Whether she has a covenant head or not was not worth considering.* The fact that a man has taken a solemn vow assuming covenantal responsibility for his offspring was judged by our highest court to be a matter of no legal consequence.

It is difficult to understand what is more tragic, the decision of the Court to slaughter the children or the inability of modern Christians to even notice that the Court had declared every child in the nation to be, as far as they were concerned, a covenant bastard.

With this abortion decision, the rejection of the legal reality of family covenants finally came to the shedding of blood. But they are God's judgment on us. *We* do not see either.

Having been exhorted by somebody to "get involved," we think the solution is to "throw the bums out." But the "bums" are simply the hand of the Lord upon us; the only way out is repentance. The only safe way to flee from the Lord is to turn *to* Him. The Lord says, "I will give children to be their princes, and babes shall rule over them. The people will be oppressed, every one by another and every one by his neighbor; the child will be insolent toward the elder, and the base toward the honorable" (Is. 3:4–5). The Lord is angry with us, and we see results on every hand: "As for My people, children are their oppressors, and women rule over them. O My people! Those who lead you cause you to err, and destroy the way of your paths" (Is. 3:12). And as a people, we do not yet see the causes of His just judgment upon us.

Repentance must begin in each household with husbands and fathers turning from their effeminacy. Tragically, much of our current folly is effeminacy in the name of Christ. Contrary to popular teaching on the Christian home, a man's duty is not be a real sweet guy, well-liked by all at church. Much of the effort being expended on masculine renewal today is nothing more than a discipleship program for weenies—a pale copy of the secular men's movement of a few years back. In contrast, a husband must assume a mantle of strength and the demeanor of masculine leadership. And when men have assumed godly responsibility within the home, they must then bring that representative headship to bear outside the home. This is the real test. A man who thinks he leads at home but has a failure of nerve as the family's ambassador will have no more cultural impact than the average bossy college roommate.

In this way our repentance can spread first to the church, as it is given an opportunity to receive the heads of covenant households in their official representative capacity for the first time in generations. As the church is reformed in this way, it will have its former and long-forgotten strength restored. And then a biblical pattern will finally be displayed that may be safely imitated in the civil realm. But until then, all attempts at cultural reform are nothing but "all pigs fed and ready to fly."

Who will dwell in prosperity in our land? Who will inherit the earth? "The secret of the Lord is with those who fear Him, and He will show them His covenant" (Ps. 25:14). But we do not yet fear Him, and He has not yet been pleased to grant to us the great reformation of a covenant renewal. May God have mercy.

Women in Combat

Because we do not tend to think in a unified fashion (which is really a delicate way of saying that we do not think like Christians), many of the issues which perplex us seem to be unrelated to one another. But it is astonishing how many particular things can go wrong in a culture simply because the men of that culture do not have backbone.

Consequently, in times like ours, it is not surprising that women in combat is a delicate subject—but it really ought not to be. The difficulty we have in discussing the issue is really a demonstration of the problem in its own right. That problem is the fundamental capitulation to feminist norms and standards which has occurred in our culture, both within the Church and outside it. The capitulation occurred first in the home, then in the church, and finally in the cockpits of our fighter planes.

The beginning of any honest treatment of the subject must be a frank admission that, when measured by our contemporary standards, the Bible is a sexist book. This would be a bad thing if sexism were truly a sin, but in the world God made, that is not the case. When weighed in the balances of modernity, the Bible is certainly a "sinful" book. But the only thing distressing about this is that so many Christians are embarrassed by the Bible.

However, to make such an affirmation does not demonstrate in any way a hostility to women. Misogyny, or hatred of women, *is* a sin and is flatly prohibited to all followers of Christ. Husbands are required to love their wives in the same way that Christ loved the church (Eph. 5:25), and the apostle Peter instructs men to take special care to honor their wives (1 Pet. 3:7). A godly man is one who rises in the gates of the city and blesses the name of his wife (Prov. 31:28). A man who finds a godly wife has found a treasure, far beyond the price of all rubies.

Clearly this is unabashed "sexism." So what is meant by an admission? No one is maintaining that it is biblically acceptable for men to mistreat women. However, a debate does exist on what exactly *constitutes* mistreatment. The debate over women in combat exists precisely because two groups of people are appealing to two different codes of law. Christians appeal to the Bible in order to define what constitutes mistreatment of women. Secularists appeal to humanistic wisdom, which, in its current form, opposes certain kinds of mistreatment.

With regard to the issue of women in combat, has there been injustice or mistreatment when a woman is excluded from a combat post, simply and solely because she is a woman? One side thinks the answer is obviously *yes*. The other side, which is represented here, denies it.

Christians should routinely turn to their Bibles to settle such questions, and on this subject, the Bible is clear. To keep women out of combat is nothing more than simple, biblical prudence because women as a group are not suited for combat. Put another way, women do a poor job fighting. The fact that the Bible is so infrequently quoted in this debate is less an indication of a genuine scriptural silence than a real indication of how little we want biblical answers for our problems.

When Isaiah the prophet is declaring the judgment of the Lord against Egypt, he speaks of their fears in this way: "In that day *Egypt will be like women, and will be afraid* and fear because of the waving of the hand of the LORD of hosts, which He waves over it. And the land of Judah will be a terror to Egypt; everyone who makes mention of it will be afraid in himself, because of the counsel of the LORD of hosts which He has determined against it" (Is. 19:16–17).

Jeremiah speaks in the same way: "A sword is against the soothsayers, and they will be fools. A sword is against her mighty men, and they will be dismayed. A sword is against their horses, against their chariots, and against all the mixed peoples who are in her midst; *and they will become like women*. A sword is against her treasures, and they will be robbed" (Jer. 50:36–37).

A chapter later, the same prophet uses the same comparison: "And the land will tremble and sorrow; for every purpose of the LORD shall be performed against Babylon, to make the land of Babylon a desolation without inhabitant. The mighty men of Babylon have ceased fighting, they have remained in their strongholds; *their might has failed, they became like women*; they have burned her dwelling places, the bars of her gate are broken" (Jer. 51:29–30). Measured by our contemporary standards, Nahum is no better: "Surely, *your people in your midst are women!* The gates of your land are wide open for your enemies; fire shall devour the bars of your gates" (Nah. 3:13).

When these passages are considered together, we should conclude that a standard way for the prophets of God to tell a people that their military might has failed them is to say that their warriors have come to the point where they fight like women. A legitimate conclusion from this would be that if it is a bad thing to have your men fight like women, then surely it would be a bad thing to have your women fight like women.

The assumption throughout all Scripture is that men go to war. When the men of Israel are numbered for war, the count is made of all men twenty years old and above—"Take a census of all the congregation of the children of Israel, by their families, by their fathers' houses, according to the number of names, *every male* individually, from twenty years old and above—*all who are able to go to war* in Israel. You and Aaron shall number them by their armies" (Num. 1:2–3).

This is not offered up as some kind of biblically-based insult to women. It is certain that insults are being used in the earlier passages cited, but the insult is not directed at women at all. The insult is directed at the warriors, who are described in those places as fighting like women.

But how is it *not* an insult to women when their

characteristics are used insultingly against men? The answer is a simple one, but we have to make a basic distinction between direct insults and comparative insults first.

A direct insult would be to say that someone is ugly, or that some workmanship is slipshod. The negative description stands on its own and does not need any further context to make the meaning plain . . . and the meaning is derogatory.

But a comparative insult is to take the characteristics of one thing, which are fitting for that thing, and apply them to something else which ought not to have those characteristics. When we say that something flies like a lead balloon, we are not trying to insult lead, which has many admirable attributes in other settings. We are simply maintaining that it does not have balloon-like characteristics.

So which is superior, a ten-pound sledge, or a china tea cup? The answer depends entirely on what you want to do. Do you want to drink tea or drive in railroad spikes? To ascribe to a railroad spike the attributes of delicacy and beauty would be to insult that railroad spike (not that it would care). It would not be an insult to the attributes of delicacy and beauty themselves.

The Bible tells us that women are not as good as men are in the important work of violence. Men have one kind of strength and women have another. The strength of each domain becomes a weakness outside of that domain. No man should want to be told that he throws hand grenades like a girl. And no mother should want to be told that she rocks her child to sleep like a team of Navy Seals.

Clearly, the Bible is insulting warriors when it identifies them as a bunch of women, but the insult can only be understood if the strengths of women in another realm are equally understood. The issue of women in politics did not arise because the Joint Chiefs of Staff were clamoring for just such a reform in order to improve their military efficiency. Rather, the dubious policy was forced on them from outside. Tragically, our military leaders, who ought to be noted for their courage, have shown little of it in this situation; timidity and cowardice have been the order of the day. Ironically, this entire debacle provides us with a *modern* instance of our warriors becoming like women.

Because of the growth of feminism in our culture generally, women have risen to positions of influence in our civil realm. While the Bible does not prohibit women in civil leadership *per se*—the instance of Deborah comes to mind—the Bible does say that when feminine leadership is common, it should be reckoned not as a blessing but as a curse—"As for My people, children are their oppressors, and women rule over them. O My people! Those who lead you cause you to err, and destroy the way of your paths" (Is. 3:12).

Because feminism is rampant in our time, women have been thrust into positions they are not naturally suited for. These positions include many positions of responsibility in the civil realm. Because we do not live in a military dictatorship, these feminist inroads into the civil realm have in turn placed feminist women, and those influenced by their feminism, in a position where they can begin dictating to the military what they ought to be doing. Because the feminist mind works differently, the goal of the military is no longer seen in terms of military efficiency (e.g., destruction of the enemy), but rather as a laboratory for social engineering in which women can be accepted and learn how to feel good about themselves.

The goal of the military ought to be that of being formidable in battle, and such military efficiency is greatly diminished by the presence of women. There are many reasons for this. The women provide a sexual distraction; a man in love with one of his fellow soldiers is not going to function the way he ought to in battle. The presence of women in the military tends to distort the nature of covenantal lines of authority (Eph. 5:22–25). Third, women are built by God to bear children, and pregnant women will fight even more poorly than women generally do.

Further, the logistical costs of getting pregnant women away from the front is considerable, as we have already found out in our recent experiments with women in warfare. And last, the Bible requires a straightforward system of equal weights and measures. God rejects all such double standards. But the presence of women in the military necessitates such double standards. For example, the military academies have not accepted women who could perform the physical tests that used to be required of all the men. Two sets of standards have developed, which means that a man can wash out for physical reasons and still be ahead of someone else who remains. This creates tension and hostility within the ranks and impairs military efficiency.

According to Scripture, men have a solemn responsibility to defend their homes, their wives, and their children. When a nation has finally come to the point where it is defended by the women, that same nation no longer deserves to be defended. Nehemiah once charged the men of Israel with their duty in this regard, saying, "And I looked, and arose and said to the nobles, to the leaders, and to the rest of the people, 'Do not be afraid of them. Remember the Lord, great and awesome, and fight for your brethren, your sons, your daughters, your wives, and your houses'" (Neh. 4:14). This is a duty which we must remember and embrace.

SECTION FOUR

Federal Father

Incredible Loveliness

Learning to be a federal father begins with learning to be a
federal husband for a pregnant wife. The task is attended
with tremendous blessings: "Blessed is every one who fears
the Lord, who walks in His ways. When you eat the labor
of your hands, you shall be happy, and it shall be well with
you. Your wife shall be like a fruitful vine in the very heart
of your house, your children like olive plants all around
your table. Behold, thus shall the man be blessed who fears
the Lord. The Lord bless you out of Zion, and may you see
the good of Jerusalem all the days of your life. Yes, may
you see your children's children. Peace be upon Israel!"
(Ps. 128:1–6).

Feminine beauty takes many forms, but in modern times
the most overlooked form of this blessed beauty is that of
pregnancy. Because we do not pay attention to our Bibles,
we have now come to the point where we dismiss this blessing contemptuously, or we make fun of it, or we make rude
comments to those who have received the blessing. The
result is that too often modern Christian women abhor
pregnancy because it "ruins the figure." Others lament what
happens to them because of the inconveniences involved in
getting around or in sleeping. Others associate pregnancy
with morning sickness and insist that they never want to be
pregnant again. The central problem with such opinions is

83

not that women have them but rather the context we have created, in which such opinions are formed.

This context can be described as a general bad attitude toward children and everything connected to them. Pregnancy is not honored because children are not appreciated. Unfortunately, the Christian response to this has only gone halfway back. Some men have learned that children are a blessing, and so they have decided with their wives that they want to have more kids. Sometimes this decision is reached with some reluctance, but it is reached. Nevertheless, decisions are often made on the basis of raw principle with no attitudinal follow-through. We have returned to the "duty" but not to the blessing.

We have consequently fallen down in between two positions. We have rejected the contempt the world shows for the results of pregnancy, but we have not yet learned to honor pregnancy ourselves. If a pregnant woman enters a modern gathering of Christians in the condition that Luke describes concerning our Lord's mother (i.e., great with child), the chances are good that she will hear three rude comments before the evening is out. Two people will want to pat her stomach, as though being pregnant makes one's body public property, and one person will set up shop as a wit. "Does the doctor know what causes this?" A few more serious individuals will express some concern for her, the kind of concern that baits the snare for discontent. "Is Joe taking care of you? You look awfully tired."

A world of difference lies between men who insist that women should do their duty, and men who honor women who fulfill their calling—"Nevertheless she will be saved in childbearing if they continue in faith, love, and holiness, with self-control" (1 Tim. 2:15). Women, like men, are saved by God's grace in the midst of their vocational callings. In the wisdom of God, pregnancy is the beginning of this calling for women. God gave Adam the task of being fruitful and filling the earth. But Adam was utterly incapable of reproducing by himself. He needed a helper suitable to him, someone able to help him be fruitful. And when Adam received his helper, he honored her.

Paul says that true widows are to be honored (1 Tim. 5:3). If their families cannot take care of them, then the church should help, provided they were renowned for their good works, which specifically included the rearing of children (v. 10). The calling which is honored at the end of a woman's life must also be honored at the beginning of it.

Men must learn to see pregnancy as an honor bestowed, and they must themselves honor those to whom it has been given. Men must do this generally, and husbands must do it particularly. The point is to see pregnancy as more than good, more than a duty, more than important; *this condition is lovely.* Imagine this situation: a woman, bearing within her body another eternal soul, enters a room filled with men. They all stand and greet her, and they speak of this and that. No one refers to her pregnancy, but the vast majority of them are thinking, "Now that is really something. She is incredible." Their demeanor is one of respect and honor. When men generally respect pregnant women, and husbands particularly learn to verbally respect and honor and admire their wives' loveliness in pregnancy, our situation with regard to our families will soon be very different.

In traditional conservative Christian circles, a common lament is that modern women are not eager to have children the way women were in the Bible. Women are too eager to rush off to a childless career; women are disgruntled about the calling which God has given them. But then, look at how pregnant women are treated in their midst. Why are we surprised? Why should women honor what their men treat with contempt?

When we have learned this lesson, we will be better prepared for federal thinking after the children have arrived. At the same time, additional applications will always be necessary.

Covenant Fruit

We have already seen that marriages are covenantal entities. This is no less true of the fruit of such covenantal unions. The family is not established by custom or by legislation. The family is established and defined by the Word of God alone. As we have seen the strength of a man's federal connection to his wife, we should not be surprised to find that the Bible describes a very close covenantal connection between a man and his children.

In Malachi, where wives are described as wives by covenant (2:14), we also see why God intended this covenantal union in the first place: "But did He not make them one, having a remnant of the Spirit? *And why one? He seeks godly offspring.* Therefore take heed to your spirit, and let none deal treacherously with the wife of his youth" (Mal. 2:15). The reason God brings husband and wife together in federal union is so that they might bring up godly offspring before Him. Not surprisingly, there is a deep federal connection with the children. Water does not rise above its level, and a covenantal marriage cannot bear non-covenantal fruit.

This federal understanding is very wonderfully set forward in the Bible's description of Job's understanding of his parental responsibility.

> And his sons would go and feast in their houses, each on his appointed day, and would send and invite their three sisters to eat and drink with them. So it was, when the days of feasting had run their course, that Job would send and sanctify them, and he would rise early in the morning and offer burnt offerings according to the number of them all. For Job said, "It may be that my sons have sinned and cursed God in their hearts." Thus Job did regularly. (Job 1:4–5)

In this text, Job does not offer sacrifices because of a feeling of guilt or to cover for his parental failures. This practice of his is actually being described as an example of his righteousness. In the first verse of the book, Job is described in this way: "There was a man in the land of Uz, whose name was Job; and that man was blameless and upright, and one who feared God and shunned evil" (Job 1:1). Job is blameless and upright. He was a God-fearing man who shunned evil. And then, a moment after, he is described as offering these federal sacrifices for his children. He does this because of his responsibility. But notice how far he extends his responsibilities. He stands before God on account of what *any* of his children *might* have done in their *hearts*. Job is not a man to make excuses. He does not plead ignorance before God. His ignorance is what makes him sacrifice in the way that he does. It does not absolve him of responsibility at all.

As mentioned before, this is a hard concept for modern men to grasp. Fathers frequently struggle with the issues surrounding personal responsibility, because the individualism leads them to think of responsibility as *either/or*, instead of thinking *both/and*. Remember the earlier example of billiard balls which cannot occupy the same place. But this is governed by the laws of the covenant and not by the laws of physics. Covenants are hierarchical and responsibilities with them overlap. Federal responsibility of this kind does not divide but multiplies and ascends. Certain key principles are essential in order to come to understand this.

The assumption of covenant responsibility by a father does not diminish the personal responsibility of each child for everything he does and thinks; rather, it strengthens it. A father must beware the false dichotomy between individualism and "patriarchalism." The individualist says to each person in the family that responsibility begins and ends with him. Only one person can be responsible for one thing. The "patriarchalist" approach would agree and then say that the only person responsible in the family is the Boss Man. If he is responsible, then no one else can ever *do* anything freely. Both approaches are erroneous.

Federal thinking in the household is a point of unity.

Apart from this covenantal thinking, adversarial thinking will necessarily develop in the family. A husband sees himself on one side, and his wife sees herself on the other. Each has a perspective and thinks its right. Again, covenantal thinking is the biblical basis for being able to say *we* and for having that pronoun mean something in the throne room of God.

The federal mind is not a technique; it is a mind of wisdom. A man must always be careful to distinguish application from mindless conformity. A man can say, "I am the federal head of this place," every morning when he gets up, but covenant mantras do not work any better than any other kind of mantra. Too many people want twelve steps, or seven steps, or three steps out of their problems, and this approach cannot be manipulated in this fashion.

Anti-covenantal, pietistic thinking works this way: "I caught my son reading *Penthouse*. That's not how we taught him. He should know better. How could he . . ?" Now that the father knows about the sin, he thinks he is responsible to say something, but he was responsible *before* he knew. This mindset thinks that knowledge brings a measure of personal responsibility—the responsibility to exhort another about *his* responsibilities. But as that clever unbeliever Ambrose Bierce noted, exhortation is the practice, in religious affairs, of putting the conscience of another onto a spit and roasting it to a nut brown discomfort. In this scenario, a father uses his knowledge as a weapon against his child. When the father says nothing, the child drifts away. When the father says something, he drives the child away.

But covenantal thinking works this way: "Father, it may be that lust has a foothold in our home. We come before You in the name of Jesus Christ . . ." This transaction is accomplished *before the Lord*. Of course, a man must teach and instruct. But the issues of federal responsibilities must be deep in his bones before he undertakes any such instruction.

Cultivating this mentality will help address many problems in the household. Now in addressing "common sins" of the household, it would be easy to focus on those common sins which everyone knows and acknowledges to be sins—complaining, fighting, etc. But the point rather is to take a step or two back and address some of the problems which set up the temptations for the garden variety sins. And, as should be plain by now, the "set up" sins involve a rejection of a father's federal responsibility.

Cultivating the Roots

We often deal with sins only when they bear fruit at the branch's extremities. A lot of spiritual energy could be spared if we were willing to consider some of the root problems.

Many fathers are guilty of personal and spiritual neglect. But those who do not know the condition of their own souls are in no position to shepherd the souls of others—"Now the ones that fell among thorns are those who, when they have heard, go out and are *choked with cares*, riches, and pleasures of life, and bring no fruit to maturity" (Luke 8:14). Fathers must take care that they do not neglect the state of their own souls. "How is it with you and God?" Busyness is not holiness. Many men, even though they are not wealthy or secular hedonists, are choked with cares. They do not have the time to bring their children before the Lord in prayer.

Other men, often with enthusiastic help from their wives, exhibit what might be called defensive isolationism. In the name of having a strong family, they simply create an isolated family. But notice how Paul gives an exhortation to family members at Colossae: "Wives, submit. . . . Husbands, love. . . . Children, obey. . . . Fathers, do not provoke" (Col. 3:18–21). The point here is not the content of Paul's exhortations, but rather to note that they are given in the context of the *church*. We live in a community; the church is not a club of isolated individuals. This means that we are involved in one another's lives, which in turn means that we know one another's children.

Many parents falsely assume that they know their children better than anyone else in the church. It would be more accurate to say that parents *could* know their children better if they studied the Word, and their children, with biblical wisdom. If they did, then they would know that "faithful are the wounds of a friend, but the kisses of an enemy are deceitful" (Prov. 27:6). But many parents have fallen into a defensive posture—"my kid can do no wrong, etc."—and no one can tell them any different.

Other fathers are not prickly and defensive for the simple reason that they have prepared all their defenses beforehand. They have isolated themselves to such an extent that accountability with other Christian households becomes a virtual impossibility. This is an ignorant isolationism. Just as sin seeks out the darkness (Jn. 3:19), so sin, on the same principle, seeks *lack of accountability*. But Paul is blunt in his application of a contrasting biblical   principle, "For we dare not class ourselves or compare ourselves with those who commend themselves. But they, measuring themselves by themselves, and comparing themselves among themselves, *are not wise*" (2 Cor. 10:12). This is a common problem among those who homeschool. Consequently, when problems arise, they are not often identified until it is too late to do anything about it.

Of course a foolish homeschooling father would not fix the problem by enrolling his kids in a Christian school. *That* would lead to the problem of presumption. Far from neglecting community, this is a sin which relies entirely on "community." "All we have to do," it is thought, "is enroll our children in a good Christian school, attend a good church, and everything will turn out all right." *No, it won't.* When parents do not exercise godly and wise oversight with their children, bad things regularly and routinely happen, regardless of the community in which the children live, and regardless of the school they attend.

Other fathers want to fix their family by trifling with external things. Consequently they are suckers for the latest thing; they are constantly chasing after fads. But Paul forbids this as well—"that we should no longer be children, tossed to and fro and carried about with every wind of doctrine, by the trickery of men, in the cunning craftiness of deceitful plotting, but, speaking the truth in love, may grow up in all things into Him who is the head—Christ" (Eph. 4:14–15).

These fads we may divide into two categories—those which fit this description from Ephesians exactly and are *necessarily* destructive in their effects is the first. All antibiblical legalisms would fit into this category. "You are not *really* a genuinely committed father unless you . . . fulfil every commandment that our association of cracked brains can come up with"—you name it—godliness through beekeeping, holiness through teetotalism, righteousness through smashing your television, and onward, into the fog!

This problem with fads can also include those things which could be fruitful and constructive *if approached with wisdom*—courtship, homeschooling, and the rest of it. But stampedes never bring wisdom. Bringing up children is like working on a concrete pour, and as anyone who has worked with concrete can tell you, after forty-five minutes, you are all done. Time is a key element in this task, and after that time has passed, the thing is *done*.

Recognizing Problems

"You know you have a problem when . . ." One of the greatest wastes of time is that of fixing problems which people do not believe they have. Before a father will assume responsibility for the condition of his children before the Lord, he must know that he has a need for the teaching of Scripture. He must know that he needs God's *standards*, and he must know he needs God's *grace*. So biblically, a man should know he has a problem and needs to learn God's standards and grace, when . . .

. . . his children are routinely disobedient—"Chasten your son while there is hope, and do not set your heart on his destruction" (Prov. 19:18); "He who spares his rod hates his son, but he who loves him disciplines him promptly" (Prov. 13:24). A key word in this last verse is *promptly*. Delayed obedience is disobedience. Refusal to discipline at the time of the first offense is the same as teaching disobedience.

. . . his children roll their eyes when he tries to instruct them— "My son, keep your father's command, and do not forsake the law of your mother" (Prov. 6:20; *cf.* 4:1–4; 13:1). When children disrespect their parents' wisdom ("Oh, mom!"), there is a serious problem in the home.

. . . he finds himself making excuses for his children to others. The excuses take two forms—apologetic and defensive. Now the temptation to excuse comes from the nature of the problem—"A wise son makes a glad father, but a foolish son is the grief of his mother" (Prov. 10:1). When parents are grieved over their children, they do not necessarily think straight—"My son, be wise, and make my heart glad, that I may answer him who reproaches me" (Prov. 27:11). The proverbial "mama bear" tendency to take up the kid's part without all the facts is a great destroyer of children. In the same way, when a parent makes the apology which the *child* should make, the child is also greatly harmed. He needs to learn to eat his own cooking.

. . . he is exasperated and frustrated in his children— "Correct your son, and he will give you rest; yes, he will give delight to your soul" (Prov. 29:17). Is a man beside himself? Then *he* is disobedient. When the home is running the way it ought to run, the home is full of *rest* and *delight*.

. . . his children are whiners—"Train up a child in the way he should go, and when he is old he will not depart from it" (Prov. 22:6). How should they live and work when they are grown? They should "do all things without complaining and disputing" (Phil. 2:14). This is a hard lesson.

So when should we start learning it?

. . . his children are insecure in their masculine and feminine identity and callings, respectively—"male and female He created them" (Gen. 1:27). We are not gender-neutral material until we are called upon to assume our stations as husbands or wives. Prior to that time we are learning and preparing for that time.

. . . his children are lazy—"A wise servant will rule over a son who causes shame, and will share an inheritance among the brothers" (Prov. 17:2); "He who gathers in summer is a wise son; he who sleeps in harvest is a son who causes shame" (Prov. 10:5). Work is harder because of the Fall, but it was not caused by the Fall.

. . . his children are miserable because he doesn't love them through discipline—"For whom the Lord loves He corrects, just as a father the son in whom he delights" (Prov. 3:12). A father may have confused his sentimentalism with a biblical love for his children. But any attitude a father has which does not discipline *is not love* but some sort of destructive counterfeit. Men who do not discipline their children have contempt for them.

Now of course, no parents can say that they have perfect children in any of these areas. We are all descended from Adam; there is no getting around it. But if any of these are *characteristic* of a household, then that home is *failing* in its covenantal obligations.

Bringing up our children is a covenantal obligation. Because we are Christians, we know that no covenant is kept by our works. Rather, this covenant, like all others, is kept by Christ and is appropriated by us by faith. This means that parents must receive *grace* by faith. Now the faith that appropriates is a faith which also works, but the work performed by this faith is not the basis of your children "turning out." *That* is offered by the grace of God. Do you *believe* it? "But the mercy of the Lord is from everlasting to everlasting on those who fear Him, and His righteousness to children's children, to such as keep His covenant, and to those who remember His commandments to do them" (Ps. 103:17–18).

Nurturing Differences

In keeping with the theme of this book—the issue of masculinity—a few things should be said about training and shaping the masculinity and femininity of children. As a man brings his children up before the Lord, the distinctions between sons and daughters should become increasingly obvious—both to the parents and to the rest of the world. Three weeks after birth, "Is it a boy or girl?" is a reasonable question. Fifteen years later, the same question indicates trouble.

Our goal is to be neither "traditional" nor "modern" but rather *biblical*. That said, the human race has discovered certain things over the centuries (like the fact that grass grows up, not down), and this includes the truth that boys and girls are different. Modern egalitarian thought is therefore suspect on two counts—as a fad, it is more likely to be wrong, and as a modern fad, we are more likely to be affected by it. At the same time, Scripture is authoritative over all human observations, no matter how old.

In talking about boys and girls, men and women, we will admittedly generalize. Though generalizing is sometimes wrong in individual cases, it can be noble and necessary (Mt. 23:1ff; Tit. 1:12).

A wise father allows for variations of personality among his boys and among his girls—"So the boys grew. And Esau was a skillful hunter, a man of the field; but Jacob was a mild man, dwelling in tents" (Gen. 25:27). Masculinity and femininity are not instilled with special gender cookie cutters. The biblical mind learns to think in terms of principles and does not sweat the details.

Men are called to glorify God through the work they are called to do in the world (Gen. 2:15). With regard to

their families, men are called to *protection* and *provision*—
"And I looked, and arose and said to the nobles, to the leaders, and to the rest of the people, 'Do not be afraid of them.
Remember the Lord, great and awesome, and fight for your
brethren, your sons, your daughters, your wives, and your
houses'" (Neh. 4:14). And the Bible also says, "But if anyone does not provide for his own, and especially for those
of his household, he has denied the faith and is worse than
an unbeliever" (1 Tim. 5:8). Boys should therefore be prepared to protect and provide. This means that boys must
be taught the toughness that fights and the toughness that
takes responsibility for *providing* work.

Women are called to serve and help a man—"And the
Lord God said, 'It is not good that man should be alone; I
will make him a helper comparable to him'" (Gen. 2:18).
And Paul says, "For man is not from woman, but woman
from man. Nor was man created for the woman, but woman
for the man" (1 Cor. 11:8–9). Women must work hard as
well (Prov. 31), but it is not the work of responsible provision. Rather, it is the work of responsible service and man-
agement. This means that girls, like boys, should be brought
up to their adult callings.

The Bible requires that boys and girls present a different appearance (Deut. 22:5; 1 Cor. 11:14). As discussed
earlier, Scripture does *not* give us a detailed dress code. But
it does insist that *we* have a dress code which is not androgynous. We should not make surface judgments,
absolutizing any part of our culture. Nevertheless we are
required *to have and defend* a culture which distinguishes
male and female. While nobody in Bible times wore dresses
and trousers, we are supposed to be reflecting sexual differences in how we dress. Though a father shouldn't stress
about all the details, he should be zealous for godly distinctions.

This issue also affects how children go to school. Two
aspects of a child's education are important to consider.
The first is simple literacy, which gives access to the Word

of God. Christians are to be people of the Word, so we should insist that our children be people of *words*. We are Christians, so we love books. A second aspect comes under the heading of the cultural mandate and consists of our *exercising dominion* in the various areas to which God has called us. God has not called us to sit around in the world. He has called us to study it and subdue it. This requires a rigorous education. The obvious limits to this should be God-given and not *self*-determined. A refusal to educate your daughters is a refusal to educate your grandsons—and that grants dominion to God-haters.

A big issue for many fathers is the question of athletics. Every time we go through another round of the Olympics, we see the humanistic religion of modernity in its full regalia. Do not let the world dictate to you what you "must" do. Athletics are certainly lawful (1 Cor. 9:24–27), and they are certainly lawful for girls. But do not let the modern athletic mandate set aside requirements of *modesty* or the standards of *feminine propriety*.

Disciplining Discipline
All of the above sections assume a framework of discipline, and behind all our nurturing and chastening we have to get very clear on the *principles* which underlie consistent biblical discipline. Though I've discussed childrearing in more detail in *Standing on the Promises*, here I expand upon those principles within the explicit context of federal fatherhood, emphasizing certain aspects in response to recent discussions.

To begin, a father should not be distracted with methods of discipline. Although biblical methods and biblically consistent methods are important, the most important thing to understand about disciplining your children is the principles which the Bible teaches on the subject.

Discipline must be *confident*—"Foolishness is bound up in the heart of a child; the rod of correction will drive it far from him" (Prov. 22:15). God attaches *promises* to discipline when the discipline is applied the way He instructs. To apply discipline without believing his promises is impudence. The impudence can take various forms—anxiety, overt unbelief, etc. Many parents will say, "We tried that but it didn't work." First, what does this mean, "We *tried* obedience"? And secondly, it did not work because the form of religion without the substance of religion never does work. The word *confident* literally means "with faith." Your children must be disciplined in faith, through faith, and *from faith*. A federal father must search out and cling to God's promises concerning discipline.

And, of course, discipline must be *affectionate*—"And you have forgotten the exhortation which speaks to you as to sons: My son, do not despise the chastening of the LORD, nor be discouraged when you are rebuked by Him; for whom the LORD loves He chastens, and scourges every son whom He receives" (Heb. 12:5–6). The author of Hebrews compares divine discipline with human discipline. One of the points of comparison is that discipline represents love, affection, and identification. A man who refuses to discipline his son is, in effect, disinheriting him. This rejection, or hatred, is utterly contrary to the attitude Christian parents are to have toward their children. Affectionate discipline gives the children something to return to after repentance.

Discipline must be *judicial*—"Brethren, if a man is overtaken in any trespass, you who are spiritual restore such a one in a spirit of gentleness, considering yourself lest you also be tempted" (Gal. 6:1). When there has been a trespass in any situation, the ones who are qualified to deal with it are those who are *spiritual*. In the home, this results in a common catch. A father is qualified to discipline when he does not "feel like it." And when he emotionally "feels like it," he is not qualified. Discipline of the child must therefore begin with *self*-discipline.

Discipline must be *swift*—"Do not be deceived, God is not mocked; for whatever a man sows, that he will also reap" (Gal. 6:7). But as God governs the world, not uncommonly, considerable time elapses between the sowing and the reaping. So a godly father should remember he is not just exercising the principle, he is *teaching* the principle to young minds. Consequently, the time between sowing and reaping should be as short as possible. Even the youngest infant understands causation at some level, but the younger the child the more immediately he should be disciplined. The Bible teaches this, "He who spares his rod hates his son, but he who loves him disciplines him *promptly*" (Prov. 13:24).

Discipline must be *painful*—"Now no chastening seems to be joyful for the present, but painful" (Heb. 12:11a). If the discipline is *not* painful, then it does not qualify as discipline. The tenderness of parents, particularly of mothers, is a common point of stumbling. This tenderness which refuses to discipline is a "kindness" which kills. God has required us to inflict pain on those who are dear to us. The pain involved in godly discipline is both *positive* and *negative*.

Swift, painful discipline does not mean the father is to be an ogre but just the reverse. We see from Proverbs 3:11–12 that discipline from the Lord requires comfort and encouragement afterwards. If this is the case with divine discipline, how much more is it necessary when our earthly parents correct us? "As a father pities his children, so the Lord pities those who fear Him. For He knows our frame; He remembers that we are dust" (Ps. 103:13–14).

The Bible is blunt in its requirement of fathers in this regard, "Fathers, *do not provoke* your children, lest they become discouraged" (Col. 3:21). No more effective means of provocation exists than erratic, harsh, unloving, or inconsistent discipline. A man who is incapable of lovingly encouraging his children after discipline is not *qualified* to exercise any discipline at all.

The encouragement should include follow-up instruction. If any questions remain, they should be answered.

It should also include prayer. God is present and working through the discipline, and His presence should be acknowledged. The child should be assured of forgiveness. The breach of fellowship is now *gone*. As a result, there has been restoration of fellowship. A father should take special care to be warm and cheerful after discipline.

Obviously, discipline must be *effective*—"Afterward it yields the peaceable fruit of righteousness to those who have been trained by it" (Heb. 12:11b). At the same time, just because something is painful does not mean that it qualifies as discipline. Discipline is corrective, while punishment is a simple matter of justice. When the civil magistrate executes a serial killer, the point is not to improve the murderer. This is punishment, not discipline. The point in discipline is to correct and change the character and behavior of the children. If it is not having this effect, then it is not discipline. And the final harvest may be gauged from the "early returns." When a child is given a bath, you do not measure success by the amount of time spent in the tub. The success is measured by *results*. One important part of effectiveness in discipline is *consistency*.

Discipline must *reflect biblical standards*—"And in vain they worship Me, teaching as doctrines the commandments of men" (Matt. 15:9). A father should never fall into the trap of thinking that anything that is "strict" is biblical. Most false religions are strict. If a man applies discipline wrongly, he can mess with his kid's head for life. He must not confuse house rules with God's rules. He must teach his children to make such basic distinctions. God does not require that little kids keep their feet off the couch. This is a house rule. God does require that children obey their parents. This is God's rule. And that is why they must keep their feet off the couch.

Principles must be applied in order to be of any use. And when they are applied, they will take a certain shape or form. When parents discipline their children, one should always be able to see clearly the principles which are being applied.

One good way to do this is to identify clearly the sin involved. A father should remember that discipline is *teaching*. The lesson should not be, "Sometime in the recent past you have displeased me somehow or other." Rather, the lesson should be something like, "I do not object to cleaning up closets. But you must realize that when you went upstairs to do this, you were not doing what I had *told* you to do, which was to clean the basement. I appreciate the work you did on the closet, but Samuel did say to King Saul that to obey is better than sacrifice. What you did was disobedience."

The sin that was committed by the child should be identified and named. An appropriate passage of Scripture should be brought to bear. The child should be instructed by Scripture as he is being disciplined by his father. As the child is disciplined, allowances should be made for maturity issues. Allowances must never be made for *moral* issues.

At the center of all is the desire that the federal father has to teach his children to honor him and their mother. He does this not because he is power-tripping, but because he wants his children to live their lives under the blessings of God—"Honor your father and your mother, *that your days may be long* upon the land which the Lord your God is giving you" (Exod. 20:12); "Children, obey your parents in the Lord, for this is right. 'Honor your father and mother,' which is *the first commandment with promise*: 'that it may be well with you and *you may live long on the earth*'" (Eph. 6:1–3).

Although we all have a duty to honor our parents, we must honor and love God more. This is fundamental. No human government, no human relationship is absolute. All must come under our relationship to God. As Jesus taught, "He who loves father or mother more than Me is not worthy of Me. And he who loves son or daughter more than Me is not worthy of Me" (Mt. 10:37). In saying this, Christ was not setting aside God's law; rather, He was repeating it (Mt. 19:19). This is not a truth limited to our emotional lives; it affects what we *do*: "He [Ahaziah] did evil in the sight of the Lord, *and walked in the way of his father and in the way of his mother* and in the way of Jeroboam the son of Nebat, who had made Israel sin" (1 Kgs. 22:52). The Bible tells us what to do when parents are wicked. We owe our primary allegiance to God alone.

But under His authority, disobedience to the Fifth Commandment is not a "little deal." We see this first in the fact that the requirement is placed among the other nine. We also see how New Testament writers treated this sin: "For men will be lovers of themselves, lovers of money, boasters, proud, blasphemers, *disobedient to parents*" (2 Tim. 3:2). Paul includes this in Romans in a list of great forms of wickedness: "backbiters, haters of God, violent, proud, boasters, inventors of evil things, *disobedient to parents*" (Rom. 1:30). Considering the company it keeps, disobedience to parents is not a tiny sin.

Honoring parents includes many duties. First, children must be *students* of their parents—"My son, hear the instruction of your father, and do not forsake the law of your mother" (Prov. 1:8). They must have a clear desire to *please* their parents—"A wise son makes a *glad* father, but a foolish son is the grief of his mother" (Prov. 10:1; cf. 15:20; 19:26; 23:25). Corresponding to this, children must be *attentive* to their parents—"*Listen* to your father who begot you, and do not despise your mother when she is old" (Prov. 23:22). Children must also *respect the romantic responsibilities* of their parents with regard to the child's interests— "But if . . . evidences of virginity are not found for the young woman, then they shall bring out the young woman to the door of her father's house, and the men of her city shall stone her to death with stones" (Deut. 22:20–21). A father is responsible for the sexual purity of his children. His children should be receptive to his guidance and instruction in the matter.

Children have an obligation to *bless* their parents— "There is a generation that curses its father, and *does not bless* its mother" (Prov. 30:11). Obviously related, children must *revere* their parents—"Every one of you shall revere his mother and his father, and keep my Sabbaths: I am the Lord your God" (Lev. 19:3).

On a practical front, children must *repay* their parents— "But if any widow has children or grandchildren, let them first learn to show piety at home and to *repay* their parents; for this is good and acceptable before God" (1 Tim. 5:4). This is how Jesus interprets this commandment in Mark 7:10. Honoring parents includes financial commitments. This corresponds to the earlier duty parents have for their children (2 Cor. 12:14). This is one of the duties which a man should seek to perform for *his* parents to set the pattern or example for his children.

Children must *obey* their parents—"Children, obey your parents in all things, for this well pleasing to the Lord" (Col. 3:20). Clearly, children must *never strike* their parents—"And he who strikes his father or his mother shall surely be put to death" (Exod. 21:15). Equally clearly, children must *never curse* their parents— "And he who curses his father or his mother shall surely be put to death" (Exod. 21:17; cf. Lev. 20:9). And although we have been told many times in our modern world that youth is wiser than age, the Bible says that children must *never make contemptuous fun* of their parents—"The eye that mocks his father, and scorns obedience to his mother, the ravens of the valley will pick it out, and the young eagles will eat it" (Prov. 30:17). Neither should children *show any kind of contempt* for their parents—"Cursed is the one who treats his father or his mother with contempt. And all the people shall say, 'Amen!'" (Deut. 27:16).

Choosing and Taking a Wife

If a father raises his sons and daughters faithfully, then the little ones have a strange tendency to grow and finally get married down the road. As in the previous section, though I've written on these topics in *Her Hand in Marriage*, here

I expand upon some of the principles in light of the responsibilities of the federal father and in light of the ongoing dialogue about courtship.

How should a young man seek a wife? What should his criteria be? First, a few important pointers on what not to do. Do not hand out photocopies of this chapter at the college and career class at church, announcing in a loud voice that you are ready for the marital state and are earnestly praying about it. That makes godly young women jumpy; they want to get married too, but not to a blunderbuss.

Certain things should be assumed in the discussion. A man should not even consider marrying a woman who is not a Christian—"Be ye not unequally yoked together with unbelievers: for what fellowship has righteousness with unrighteousness? and what communion has light with darkness?" (2 Cor. 6:14). A man should not even consider marrying a woman who was divorced without biblical grounds (Mt. 19:9). Further, if *he* is divorced unbiblically (Mt. 19:9), then he should forget it. Simply put, before a man considers this woman or that one, he should have it resolved in his mind that he will marry only within the boundaries set by the law of God.

Beyond this, we come to the realm of wisdom; the task involves making important judgment calls. The various criteria set forth here are not ranked in hierarchichal order; they are simply considerations which should be very much a part of a young man's thinking.

Although a young man leaves his father and mother in order to take a wife (Gen. 2:24), the advice and approval of his parents should be very important to him (Gen. 28:6–9). If he is headstrong and refuses to listen to counsel, he will likely regret it in his marriage. Our culture likes to pretend that wisdom belongs to youth, especially in questions of love. The Bible teaches us to look for wisdom elsewhere. The way of a man with a maiden does not necessarily make a lot of sense (Prov. 30:18–19).

A man should seek a *pleasant* woman. The Bible has a

great deal to say about a quarrelsome wife and the constant nuisance associated with living with such a one. "The contentions of a shrewish woman are like a continuing dripping" (Prov. 19:13). Some men, who do not want the responsibilities associated with leadership, may be content to marry a woman who brings "direction" to the relationship, but a hard-driving woman is likely to be an unpleasant companion after a very short period of time.

He should want to marry a woman who shares a biblical work ethic with him; she should understand her work orientation as being homeward (Tit. 2:3–5). A woman who rejects domesticity, who wants to live like a Barbie married to Ken, should be avoided along with all other sexual pests. A biblical man should want a woman who wants children and who wants to be home-oriented.

At the same time, when a man is considering a woman, she should be sexually attractive to him. He should banish from his thinking all false gnosticism, which says that the "spiritual plane" is so much more important. Of course it is more important, but this does not make sexual attraction irrelevant. When a man singles a woman out for attention, he should have one thing clear in his mind. (Actually, a young Christian woman should understand the same thing as well.) To some extent, one of two things is happening. The first option is that the man is attempting to get the woman into bed dishonorably. The other possibility is that he is trying to do it honorably. If this sounds crass, you may not fully appreciate the holiness of the marriage bed.

But, returning to the previous point, a man has to realize that the world is full of sexually attractive women who would turn his life into a wretched affair. Although sexual chemistry is necessary for a good marriage, it is by no means sufficient—"Favor is deceitful, and beauty is vain: but a woman who fears the Lord, she shall be praised" (Prov. 31:30).

If a man and woman come from different cultures, the differences should be taken fully into account. The

tendency is to look at all such differences through a romantic haze and, if anyone brings them up, to dismiss them
with a wave of the hand. "Oh, we thought of that." But
thinking "of that" and thinking it *through* are two different
things. We cannot say that cross-cultural marriages (which
would include interracial marriages) are unbiblical. We can
say that they should not be approached thoughtlessly. The
differences between men and women are great enough already; if a couple has to deal with other cultural barriers to
communication as well, it could cause considerable problems. The same thing goes for what might be called certain
subcultural differences—vocational, regional, etc.

Last, a young man must know that the woman he is
considering respects him enough to follow his spiritual leadership. Doctrinal differences which may not seem huge in
a "conversation" may become quite large in a family when
practical decisions have to be made. For example, how would
a husband and wife handle a disagreement over infant baptism?

Because the husband is spiritually responsible in the
marriage, the young man should think all such things through
to the end *before* he puts on his courting shoes. After he
has courted and won her, they should begin thinking about
how to testify to their federal commitments in how they
come to make their covenantal vows. Few events are better
suited to highlight the federal nature of marriage than a
wedding.

Those who either blindly follow traditions or throw
traditions overboard share at least ignorance in common.
One keeps what he does not know; another throws away
what he does not know. An area where many traditions have
been lost or mindlessly kept is that of the wedding. So in
the sixties we all began to do our own thing—write our
own vows, invent our own little ceremonies, and generally
march around in our own little circle. Since then we have
settled down somewhat, but we still have the idea that the
wedding belongs to the couple and not to a culture. We

have come to believe that each wedding should be shaped by the personality of the couple, rather than our culture bestowing recognition on the couple according to the customs of our people.

What has happened to weddings has also happened in many other aspects of our cultural life with the result being an "every man to his tents, O Israel" approach. We have a horror of sameness, which is the same thing as being appalled by continuity and stability. In the midst of this chaos, some Christians have added their voices to the general babble, wanting to rethink everything and setting up their own customs for weddings from scratch.

In contrast, a far wiser course would be to defend what might be called the traditional wedding, moving toward embracing our older customs rather than innovating new ones. As always, when we consider what we are to do, we should look to the Scriptures for final authoritative guidance.

This defense of traditional weddings may be divided into three categories. The first revolves around a discovery that many elements of our traditional wedding practices have their roots in antiquity and were observed in biblical weddings of the past. The second category will be areas where we have a corresponding practice, but because we are uptight modern prigs, we do not practice these customs with the same enthusiasm. The third category includes traditions which we have not adopted or we have lost. These, if recovered, could greatly enrich our appreciation of weddings. But with this last category, such additions to the wedding ceremony should be made with extreme caution and not as individual distinctives for individual weddings. They should be brought into our weddings in some broader cultural way or not at all.

First consider the practices we have in common with scriptural weddings. A marked feature of biblical weddings is the fact that both bride and groom were gloriously attired. This was true of a royal wedding, where the bride had a gold robe (Ps. 45:13–14), and it was true of ordinary weddings. The joy and glory of wedding ornaments is used as a wonderful picture of our justification (Is. 61:10). The place and importance of bridal ornamentation is clearly assumed in the Lord's rebuke of Israel: "Can a virgin forget her ornaments, or a bride her attire? Yet My people have forgotten Me days without number" (Jer. 2:32). A bridal veil may have been a part of this attire (Gen. 24:65). At the marriage supper of the Lamb, the bride is arrayed in wonderful linen (Rev. 19:8–9). In every description of weddings given to us in Scripture, the bride is adorned (Rev. 21:2). Tuxedos and uniforms, gowns, trains and veils, are very much in keeping with how Scripture describes a wedding.

We also have the practice of having bridesmaids and friends of the groom stand with the bride and groom at the wedding. This is also a biblical practice, although in at least one instance the number of groomsmen was fairly large— "They brought thirty companions to be with him" (Judg. 14:11). Still the groomsmen were very clearly part of a biblical wedding. Jesus refers to His disciples in the figure of groomsmen (Mt. 9:15). This includes the counterpart to our custom of having a best man (Judg. 14:20; 15:2). This best man was called "the friend of the bridegroom" (Jn. 3:29); he may even have been the one who had various important responsibilities at the wedding—the master of the feast (Jn. 2:8–9). If this is the case, we have a parallel in the various duties which we assign to the best man.

But we also find some common practices which have fallen into disrepair in our day. Feasting in association with weddings was common (Gen. 29:22; Judg. 14). These feasts were not two-hour affairs, and they probably were not limited to small bowls of mints—"And he kept the wedding feast fourteen days" (Tobit 8:19). We have toned this practice down to what we call a wedding reception. In contrast, the biblical practice was to have a feast. Many moderns attend wedding receptions out of a reluctant sense of duty and not because the feasting will be glorious. This is clearly something we have to work on.

Weddings in biblical times were a cultural voice of gladness. A terrible judgment was promised to Judah when God said that this mirth, the voice of the bride and groom, would be removed from the land (Jer. 7:34). In the extracanonical book of 1 Maccabees, we find a wedding party described in the course of some fighting—"Where they lifted up their eyes, and looked, and, behold, there was much ado and great carriage: and the bridegroom came forth, and his friends and brethren, to meet them with drums, and instruments of musick" (1 Macc. 9:37–41, KJV). "And Jesus said to them, 'Can the friends of the bridegroom fast while the bridegroom is with them? As long as they have the bridegroom with them they cannot fast'" (Mk. 2:19; Mt. 9:15). This wedding feasting included some good music—"Fire devoured their young men, and their maidens had no marriage song" (Ps. 78:63, RSV).

Christ in His teaching assumed that special wedding garments were not limited to the couple. All who came to a wedding had special clothing—"How did you get in here without a wedding garment?" (Mt. 22:1–14). One area where we could improve in this regard would be by getting rid of our very common practice of making bridesmaids' dresses as frumpy as possible, in what might be an attempt to make the bride look better. In a biblical ceremony, all are dressed appropriately—bride and groom, members of the wedding party, and guests.

Our weddings frequently have a toast to the bride and groom at the reception. This could perhaps be improved if we self-consciously named the toast what it really is—a blessing—"And they blessed Rebekah and said to her: 'Our sister, may you become the mother of thousands of ten thousands; and may your descendants possess the gates of those who hate them'" (Gen. 24:60). We also see the beautiful blessing given to Boaz and Ruth: "The Lord make the woman who is coming to your house like Rachel and Leah, the two who built the house of Israel" (Ruth 4:11). This blessing could be incorporated into the wedding ceremony or at the feast afterward. The blessing would come from the families of both the bride and groom.

Changes and suggested reforms should be adopted very cautiously, if at all, but perhaps a few alterations might help make things more clear. We have various symbolic gestures in our wedding ceremonies—our older custom of exchanging rings and newer innovations like the unity candle. A custom which we do not practice, which would be good to recover if we could, is having some symbol of the practice of covering. In the following passages, the phrases "under your wing," and "spread My wing," refer to the practice of spreading a garment over the bride: "And he said, 'Who are you?' So she answered, 'I am Ruth, your maidservant. Take your maidservant under your wing, for you are a close relative'" (Ruth 3:9). When God spoke of taking Israel as a bride, he used this same picture of covering as a sign of covenantal protection and security: "When I passed by you again and looked upon you, indeed your time was the time of love; so I spread My wing over you and covered your nakedness. Yes, I swore an oath to you and entered into a covenant with you, and you became Mine, says the Lord God" (Ezek. 16:8). For a hypothetical example, this might be done with a quiet eloquence if the groom had some sort of special wedding cloak which he used to cover his bride after the exchange of vows.

The Jews had another custom with their weddings which we are unlikely to revive any time soon (and I am *not* advocating it), but the principle concerning it should be recovered. In biblical times, the newly wedded couple did not head off to a motel room in another state; they were escorted to the bridegroom's chamber which was established right there on the grounds—"Which is like a bridegroom coming out of his chamber" (Ps. 19:5; Joel 2:16; Gen. 29:23; Tobit 7:16–8:1). No one wants a return to consummation on the wedding premises, but there is a principle which does need to be recovered—an abandonment of Victorian prudishness. A marriage covenant is a public covenant fence built around a private sexual relationship. In a biblical wedding, Christians should crowd into the church to witness the vows which mark the beginning of a life of faithful lovemaking. Those who struggle with even saying this would have had real trouble at covenant weddings in the Old Testament where the groom escorted his bride into his chamber at the wedding to general applause and cheering by the guests. We need to grow up a little.

Lastly, conspicuous by its absence, we do not see in biblical weddings a sacerdotal proclamation by some minister which makes a man and woman "husband and wife." The sooner we lose this foolishness the better. The church has an important role to play in witnessing the vows, and a minister may with propriety declare the vows to have been made, but the minister is no priest and marriage-maker. The couple do not stand before him to be transubstantiated.

All the governments established by God have a role to play in witnessing this covenant. Because marriage involves property, the civil authority should have a witness at all weddings, and each wedding should be registered with the magistrate—but not licensed by the magistrate. In the same way, the church must witness each wedding and may administer the vows at the wedding, but the church "creates" nothing at a wedding. Christ is the Lord of weddings.

This closing focus on weddings brings us back to the theme with which I began. Christ embraced His bride covenantally, and husbands are commanded to love their wives *as Christ loved the Church*. My point has been to show that this means that our theology of Christ's love will determine how we love our wives. If a man's theology is truly biblical and thus federal, then he will indeed love his wife as Christ loves the Church—"the holy city, New Jerusalem, coming down out of heaven from God, prepared as a bride adorned for her husband" (Rev. 21:2).